A Decade of Social Protection Development in Selected Asian Countries

This work is published under the responsibility of the Secretary-General of the OECD. The opinions expressed and arguments employed herein do not necessarily reflect the official views of OECD member countries.

This document and any map included herein are without prejudice to the status of or sovereignty over any territory, to the delimitation of international frontiers and boundaries and to the name of any territory, city or area.

Please cite this publication as:
OECD (2017), *A Decade of Social Protection Development in Selected Asian Countries*, OECD Publishing, Paris.
http://dx.doi.org/10.1787/9789264272262-en

ISBN 978-92-64-27225-5 (print)
ISBN 978-92-64-27226-2 (PDF)

Photo credits: Cover © Davidson951/Shutterstock.com

Foreword

The OECD/Korea Policy Centre held its 11th Social Experts meeting in October 2016. This provided the Centre with an opportunity to look back at a decade of change in social expenditures and social policy development. It is impossible to detail all such change across Asia in a concise volume such as this, but the report intends to give a flavour of the most relevant changes in the socio-economic context (Chapter 1) and illustrates social protection spending trends and coverage issues in Chapter 2. Throughout, this document highlights good policy practice of countries whose delegates have regularly attended the social expert meetings in Seoul.

Both the Asian Development Bank (ADB) and the International Labour Organization (ILO) have been active participants in the social expert meetings over the years. This volume too benefits from their contributions: Ms. Sri Wening Handayani and Florida Huelgas from the ADB contributed to the section on the Social Protection Indicator, while Florence Bonnet from the ILO has been most helpful in providing a range of employment and social protection of coverage data for Asia, and Céline Peyron Bista from ILO Bangkok prepared the text on efforts to increase social insurance coverage in Viet Nam.

This publication would not have been possible without the exchanges among experts at the meeting including: Ilkin Nazarov (Azerbaijan); Shaikh Shamsuddin Ahmed (Bangladesh); Dwi Retno Wilujeng Wahyu Utami (Indonesia); Yukiko Miura Katsumata and Kuriko Watanabe (Japan); Kyeong-Hoan Goh (Korea); Zulkarnain Ahmad Hatta (Malaysia); Suman Kumari Sharma (Nepal/Singapore); Saifur Rahman Sherani (Pakistan); and, Son Van Tran (Viet Nam), and the staff of the Health and Social Policy programme of the OECD/Korea Policy Centre: Sung-woong Ra (Director–General); Kyung Sook Cho (Director); Dong-Joon Kim; Yeon-Gyeong Kim; Hyeon-wu Kim; and Ji Eun Jang.

This report was prepared by Willem Adema, Pauline Fron, Yajna Govind, Hyunsook Kim and Junko Takezawa. We are indebted to Florence Bonnet and Céline Peyron-Bista (ILO) and Sri Wening Handayani and Florida Huelgas (ADB) for their contributions and to the OECD's Head of Social Policy for her comments on an earlier draft. Many other OECD colleagues provided assistance in finalising this report, including Nathalie Bienvenu, Lucy Hulett, Kate Lancaster and Marlène Mohier.

OECD/Korea Policy Center

The Joint OECD/Korea Policy Centre (http://www.oecdkorea.org) is an international co-operation organisation established by a Memorandum of Understanding between the OECD and the Government of the Republic of Korea. The Centre – officially opened on 7 July 2008 – results from the integration of four pre-existing OECD/Korea Centres, one of which was the Regional Centre on Health and Social Policy (RCHSP), established in 2005.

The major functions of the Centre are to research international standards and policies on international taxation, competition, public governance, and social policy sectors in OECD member economies and to disseminate research outcomes to public officials and experts in the Asian region. In the area of health and social policy, the Centre promotes policy dialogue and information sharing between OECD economies and non-OECD Asian/Pacific countries.

There are three main areas of work: social protection statistics (jointly with the International Labour Organization and the Asian Development Bank); health expenditure and financing statistics (jointly with the Asian Pacific National Health account Network and the World Health Organization) and on pension policies (jointly with the World Bank). In pursuit of this vision, the Centre hosts various kinds of educational programmes, international meetings, seminars, and workshops in each sector and provides policy forums presented by experts at home and abroad.

Table of contents

Tables

Figures

Acronyms and abbreviations

ADB	Asian Development Bank
ECEC	Early childhood education and care
GDP	Gross domestic product
ILO	International Labour Organization
PISA	Programme for International Student Assessment
PPP	Purchasing power parity
SME	Small and medium enterprise
SOCR	OECD Social Recipients Database
SOCX	OECD Social Expenditure Database
SPI	ADB Social Protection Indicator
STEM	Science, technology, engineering and mathematics
TFR	Total fertility rate

ISO Country Codes

ARM: Armenia	IND: India	NPL: Nepal
AUS: Australia	JPN: Japan	NZL: New Zealand
AZE: Azerbaijan	KHM: Cambodia	PAK: Pakistan
BGD: Bangladesh	KOR: Korea	PHL: Philippines
CHN: China	LAO: Lao People's Democratic Republic	PNG: Papua New Guinea
FJI: Fiji	LKA: Sri Lanka	SGP: Singapore
HKG: Hong Kong, China	MNG: Mongolia	THA: Thailand
IDN: Indonesia	MYS: Malaysia	VNM: Viet Nam

Executive summary

Over the past ten years, the socio-economic context in Asia has changed. Strong economic growth has contributed to a reduction of poverty and greater prosperity to reduced total fertility rates and increased life expectancy. Asia is increasing investment in education and its educational attainment is going up. Asia has to make the most of window of opportunity that an increasingly educated working-age population offers and prepare for the onset of population ageing in years to come.

Strong economic growth in Asia has created many new jobs, but a key issue for many Asian economies is the shortage of quality jobs. Many workers are in informal employment, which is partly the reflection of inadequate social security. Improving the job quality of workers in terms of earnings quality, labour market insecurity and the quality of the work environment will be one of Asia's major challenges in future.

While women are catching up with men in terms of educational attainment, gender employment gaps remain, especially in South Asia. Available evidence on gender pay gaps suggests these are wider in Asia than across the OECD, and can be as high as 50% at the median. Women are more likely to work in informal jobs, have no access to social protection, face vulnerable employment conditions and bear the brunt of unpaid work in and around the house.

With increasing prosperity, public social expenditure – support for households during circumstances which adversely affect their welfare – in Asia is increasing, but at 7% of GDP and 5% for non-OECD countries in Asia on average, it remains low compared to the OECD average at 21% of GDP. Furthermore in many Asian countries, including India and Indonesia, public social spending is often no higher than 2 to 3% of GDP. Low social spending is related to many (often poor) workers in Asia being in informal employment without entitlement to social protection benefits. Increasing access to social protection is key and over the past ten years China has arguably been most successful in extending coverage of social insurance programmes and public social spending increased to around 8% of GDP. However, many other economies with a large rural sector or a large urban informal sector find it very difficult to effectively increase coverage: the administrative capacity is often lacking to register participants in insurance schemes and/or collect contributions from employers and employees.

The major components of public social spending concern pensions and health, and as most of the relevant social insurance type benefits are tied to formal employment, spending is more likely to benefit non-poor households rather than poor ones, and men rather than women. Social assistance benefits may be available to the poorest households, especially if these are well targeted. However, the intensity of social assistance support may not be enough to lift households out of poverty, and many vulnerable low-income families receive very few, if any, social protection benefits. There is a growing role for non-contributory type old-age allowances and some Asian countries have established non-contributory pension schemes with widespread coverage, as the main and sometimes only system of income provision in retirement.

Spending on social assistance support is generally low, spending on labour market programmes is even lower and many low- and middle-income countries do not have a functional unemployment compensation scheme. To some extent such low expenditures are linked to strong economic growth, but the low spending levels also raise concerns on the adequacy of existing supports.

Extending social assistance and social insurance schemes is needed to reduce poverty and also provide for the increasing medical and income needs of ageing populations. Investing in children, whether or not by means of conditional cash transfers, and associated health and early and primary education services is key. Greater investment in active labour market programmes would provide the many poor and often informal workers with greater access to employment guarantee schemes and/or skill development and training.

The success of extending coverage of social insurance and other contributory schemes would ultimately rely on the ability of countries to expand productive, formal employment and increase the quality of employment in line with the principles of the OECD Job Quality Framework. The increase in average income in Asia has increased the scope for increasing public revenues, but the administrative capacity to effectively introduce and operate a contributory system of social support also needs to be developed so as to give large groups of the populations access to forms of social protection that are tied to employment. Employers, unions, and civil society also have a key role to play in promulgating coverage of social protection arrangements across Asia.

Chapter 1

The socio-economic context: A decade of growing prosperity in Asia

Over the past ten years there has been a lot change in Asia. Economic growth has contributed to a reduction of poverty as well as fertility rates, and with greater prosperity have come gains in life expectancy. In turn, this is likely to generate even greater future change as population ageing will unfold at speed, and pose considerable challenges to social and economic policy development.

Asia increasingly invests in education of its young people and in some places its young students outperform their peers in many OECD countries. This will have its effect on labour productivity in future as well as labour market relationships of employed men and women. However, at present many workers – especially women – still work in informal employment, frequently for long hours at little pay and without social protection coverage. Improving the job quality of workers in terms of earnings quality, labour market insecurity and the quality of the work environment will be one of Asia's major challenges in future.

This chapter illustrates the socio-economic gains that have been made in Asia in recent years and provides the context for the social protection expenditure trends and policy development outline in the next chapter. This chapter also presents policy examples from countries to illustrate good policy practice, including on Nutrition policy in Bangladesh, long-term care insurance in Japan, parental leave and early childhood education and care policy in Korea and efforts to increase social protection coverage in Viet Nam.

Main findings

- Over the past decade, Asian countries have experienced strong economic growth (on average 4.2% on an annual basis) and growth has been consistently strong in China and India.

- The share of people living in "absolute poverty" has fallen in most countries since 2000, and especially in Viet Nam, China and Indonesia. However, there seems to be no clear trend in income equality across Asia, since 2005.

- Asia is coming of Age. Total fertility rates have fallen to 2.2 children per women in Asia and life expectancy has increased by four years over the past decade to 73 years on average. Population ageing in Asia is expected to unfold rapidly: the old-age support ratio – the number of people of working age (15-65) per senior citizen (65+) is projected to decrease by over one-third half from 10.4 in 2015 to 6.6 by 2030.

- Educational attainment has increased by a year to 8.3 years on average across Asia. However, variation across (and within large) countries is enormous. Students from Shanghai and Hong Kong (China), and Singapore are top performers in OECD PISA test scores, while students in Indonesia, Kazakhstan and Malaysia scored below Asian and OECD averages.

- While women are catching up with men in terms of educational attainment, labour force participation rates are generally lower for women than for men and gender participation gaps are most significant in South Asian countries. Available evidence on gender pay gaps suggest these are wider in Asia than across the OECD, and can be as high as 50% at the median. Women are more likely to face vulnerable employment conditions, work in informal jobs, and therefore have less access to social protection. Women also continue to bear the brunt of unpaid work in and around the house. Improving employment conditions for women and men is one of the biggest challenges that Asia faces.

1.1. Asian countries are getting richer but growth has slowed down in 2015/16

Over the past decade, Asian countries experienced strong economic growth with higher annual growth rates (4.2% on average) than across the OECD on average (1.2%). Figure 1.1 shows that annual growth over the past ten years has been particularly strong in emerging economic powerhouses as China (9.1%) and India (6.1%), but also in economies where growth rates vary more with the price of natural resources such as Azerbaijan and Mongolia. Less affluent countries generally experienced GDP growth per capita at a relatively fast rate which reflects some evidence for catch-up growth and convergence (Figure 1.2). However, there are ample deviations from this pattern: for example, the Chinese economy grew faster than one might expect of an economy given its GDP level while the opposite held for Pakistan.

Figure 1.1. Economic growth in Asia outpaced economic growth in the OECD

GDP per capita

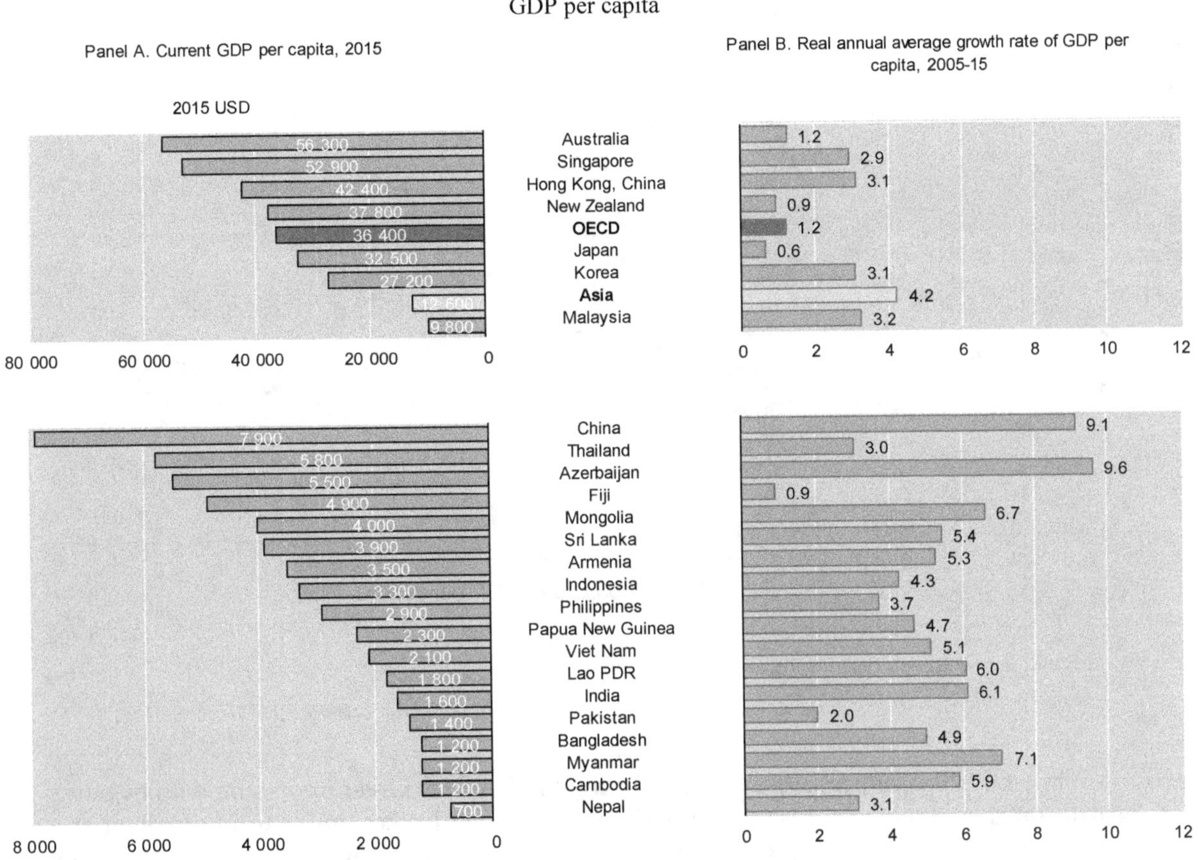

Note: The data for Myanmar is not available from 2005 to 2012.

High-income countries are defined in line with World Bank definitions, see http://data.worldbank.org/income-level/high-income. For practical reasons this figure and the figures below present data on 25 Asian countries which are deemed to represent the variety of the region rather than preparing figures with an even larger number of countries.

Source: World Bank, World Development Indicators, http://data.worldbank.org/indicator.

StatLink http://dx.doi.org/10.1787/888933457241

Most high income countries (see note to Figure 1.1) in the region also continued to experience economic growth, although at a more moderate pace: in Japan and New Zealand annual growth rates of GDP per capita were less than 1% per annum over the past ten years. GDP per capita increased by around 3% per annum in real terms in Hong Kong (China), Singapore and Korea (Figure 1.1). Income disparities in the region remain considerable (Figure 1.2): in Australia, Singapore, New Zealand, Hong Kong (China), GDP per capita is above the OECD average (USD 36 400). By contrast, GDP per capita in Nepal in 2014 was close to USD 700 and in Myanmar, Bangladesh and Cambodia it was only slightly above USD 1 000: Australia's GDP per capita is almost 90 times higher than that of Nepal.

Figure 1.2. There is some convergence in GDP per capita across Asia

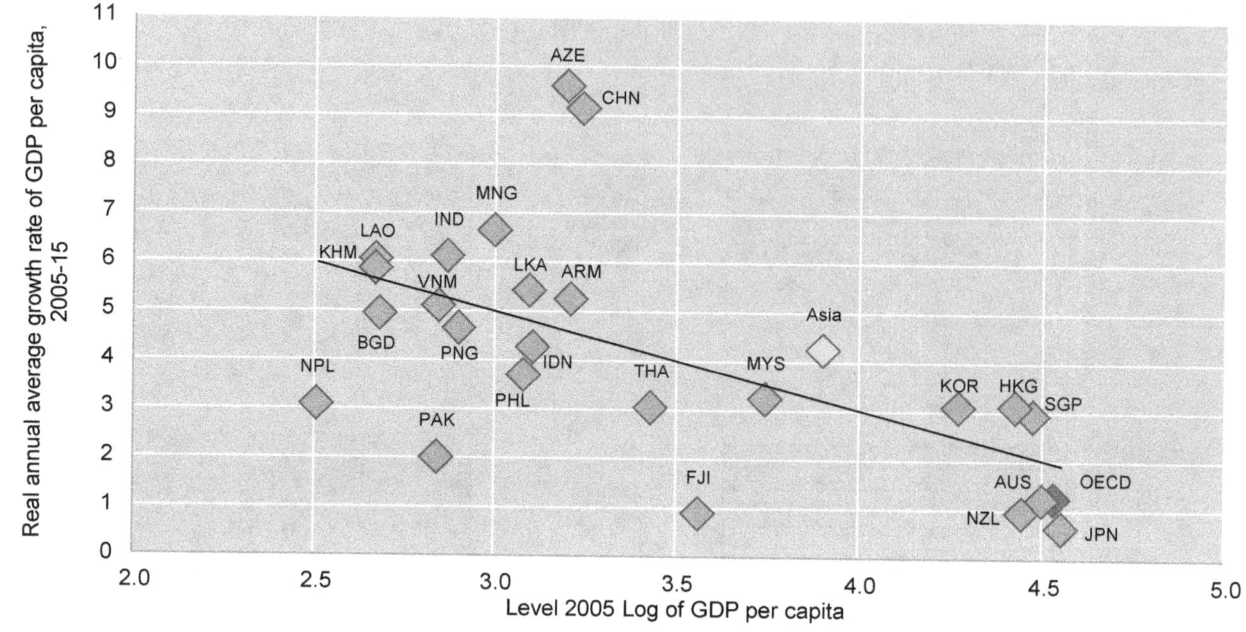

Source: World Bank, World Development Indicators, http://data.worldbank.org/indicator.

StatLink ⟶ http://dx.doi.org/10.1787/888933457251

While OECD countries were hit hard during the 2008-09 Great Recession with negative growth rates on average across the OECD, Asian economies continued to grow albeit at a reduced pace (Annex 1.A1, Figure 1.A1.1). Future economic growth rates in Asia are not expected to be as high as recently, as the world's major economies are recovering gradually, and prospects for China's future economic growth rate have been downgraded. OECD (2015) projected China's economic growth to be around 6.9% in 2016 (OECD, 2015), and ADB (2015) revised its growth rates for Asia downwards to 6.0% in 2016 – a little lower than a previous forecast. The forecasts involve a "new normal" of slower growth than experienced prior to the Great Recession.

1.2. Trends in poverty and inequality

The share of people living in absolute poverty decreased across Asia

The share of people living in "absolute poverty" – here defined as those with incomes of less than USD 2 a day – fell in most countries since 2000. Viet Nam had the largest decrease of almost 60 percentage points from 69% in 2000 to 12% in 2012, followed by China (43 percentage points) and Indonesia (39 percentage points). However, in Bangladesh, Lao PDR, India, Nepal, and Pakistan more than half of the total population still live in absolute poverty (Figure 1.3). Bangladesh has been the poorest country since 2000 and has made – compared with the other countries, limited gains in reducing absolute poverty which concerns about three-quarters of the population in 2010. However, Bangladesh has made progress with improving access to education and health as well as better nutrition, water and sanitation, although important challenges remain, particularly regarding nutrition of children and their mothers (Box 1.1).

Figure 1.3. Poverty is declining across Asia

Poverty headcount ratio at USD PPP 2 a day (% of population in selected Asian countries)

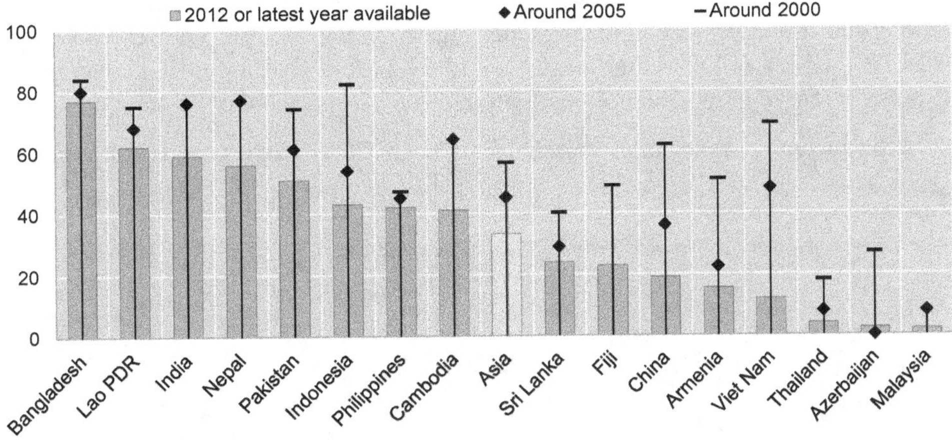

Source: World Bank, World Development Indicators, http://databank.worldbank.org/data/reports.aspx?source=world-development-indicators, as in August 2015.

StatLink http://dx.doi.org/10.1787/888933457261

Box 1.1. The Second National Plan of Action for Nutrition in Bangladesh (2016-25)

Combatting hunger and improving nutrition remain important challenges in Bangladesh despite considerable progress [for an overview, see for example, Compact 2025 (2016) and WHO (2016)]. The share of largely avoidable deaths due to disease and malnutrition has declined, as illustrated by, for example, the Child mortality rate for children 0-5 in Bangladesh which fell from almost 200 children per 1 000 births in 1980 to just below 40 in 2015 (UNICEF, 2016). Despite this achievement, Bangladesh continues to experience a high burden of malnutrition among children and adults: 18% of pregnant women are undernourished and 26% of infants have a low birth weight, and about one-third of children under 5 are underweight and/or experience stunting. Children from the lowest wealth quintile are twice as likely to be stunted as children from the highest wealth quintile (55% and 26% respectively), and such disadvantage is further worsened by seasonal variations in food availability, food price increases, gender, minority status and natural disasters. Stunting at an early age contributes to poorer cognitive and educational outcomes in later years and has significant educational and economic consequences (WHO, 2014).

In 2015, the United Nations General Assembly adopted the 2030 Agenda for Sustainable Development, which includes the goal "to end hunger, achieve food security and improved nutrition and promote sustainable agriculture (United Nations, 2016)". In order to achieve this aim, the Bangladeshi Government has developed the second National Plan of Action for Nutrition for 2016-2025 (NPAN2). This government-wide strategy is to improve the nutritional status of all, with special focus on disadvantaged groups, including mothers, adolescent girls and children (Government of Bangladesh, 2017). In terms of nutrition targets, the NPAN2 includes the following aims to be achieved (by 2025 unless otherwise specified): increase the rate of exclusive breastfeeding to over 50% in infants younger than age 6 month by 2021; reduce stunting to 25% among under-5 children by 2021; reduce the proportion of underweight among under-5 children to below 10%; and, reduce malnutrition among pregnant women and lactating mothers to below 10%.

The challenge will be to implement the strategy across 13 ministries, different administrative levels and other stakeholders and strengthen relevant programmes, including efforts to include food supply as well as dietary diversity, promotion of breastfeeding, scaling up nutrition programmes in slums and remote areas, strengthen educational programmes, including those that foster more hygienic practices, and more generally strengthen the supervision, monitoring and evaluation of the programmes. Overall, The NPAN2 is estimated to cost USD 1.6 billion over the next ten years or approximately 0.01% of GDP per annum.

For OECD countries, poverty is often measured by means of a relative income concept which defines poverty as living in a household with an equivalised household disposable household income of less than 50% of the median for the whole population (for a discussion of different concepts, see Whiteford and Adema, 2007). According to this measure, poverty rates among the four OECD countries in the region changed little, with the poverty rate in Japan (16.1%), Korea (14.6%) and Australia (13.8%) are above the OECD average (11.5%) and the poverty rate in New Zealand being around 10% (Figure 1.4).

Figure 1.4. Relative income poverty rates in Asian/Pacific OECD countries are around the OECD average

Poverty rate after taxes and transfers – poverty line at 50% of equivalised disposable household income

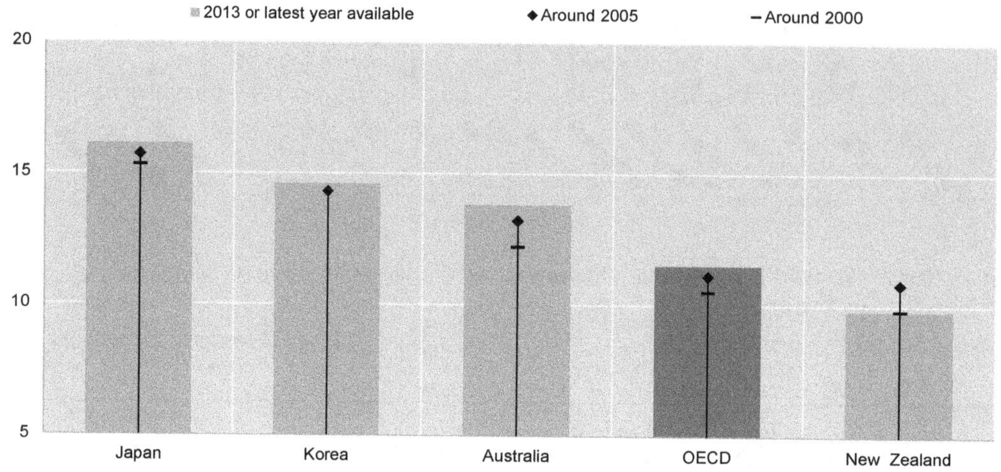

Note: The poverty rate is the ratio of the number of people (in a given age group) whose income falls below the poverty line; taken as half the median household income of the total population. The *OECD Income Distribution Database* (IDD) has been developed to benchmark and monitor countries' performance in regarding income inequality and poverty. It contains a number of standardised indicators based on the central concept of "equivalised disposable household income", i.e. total income received by households minus current taxes and transfers as adjusted for household size on basis of square root equivalence scale.

Source: *OECD Income Distribution Database* (IDD) http://www.oecd.org/social/income-distribution-database.htm.

StatLink ⟡ *http://dx.doi.org/10.1787/888933457271*

Across countries there seems to be no clear trend in income inequality

Over the past decade, income inequality measured as the Gini Coefficient decreased in many Asian countries – Armenia, Azerbaijan, Cambodia, China, the Philippines, Thailand, and Sri Lanka while large increases were recorded for Indonesia, Malaysia, and Lao PDR (for a discussion of trends over a longer time frame, see Jain-Chandra et al., 2016). Between the mid-2000s and 2013, income inequality in OECD countries in the region (Australia, Japan, Korea and New Zealand) changed little and remained close to the OECD average at 0.32. Considering a longer period – mid-1980s to 2012/13, Income inequality as measured by the Gini, increased from 0.29 to 0.32 for the 22 OECD countries for which data is available The pace of change in Australia and Japan was similar, but income inequality in New Zealand grew more rapidly from 0.27 to 0.32 (OECD, 2015b).

Among the Asian countries with rapid economic growth, China experienced an increase in income inequality until the mid-2000s, upon which income inequality declined (Figure 1.5). Shi and Peng (2015) show that since the 1980s income inequality in China increased with the privatisation of state-owned enterprises, urbanisation and migration: the population living in urban areas increased from 20% in 1980 to 55% in 2013. Strong GDP growth contributed to both the decline in poverty (as measured under different definitions) and an increase income inequality by means of rapid income growth among higher income groups in urban areas (see also Shi and Sicular, 2014). Income growth in rural areas has been faster since 2007 than before, and the recent decline in income inequality is largely due to a reduced income gap between urban and rural households from 2008 onwards as related to relatively rapid income growth among the lower income groups (see also Zhuang and Shi, 2016).

Figure 1.5. Over the last ten years there was no clear trend in income inequality in Asia

Panel A. Gini index (World Bank estimate), expenditure surveys

Panel B. OECD Gini coefficient of household disposable income

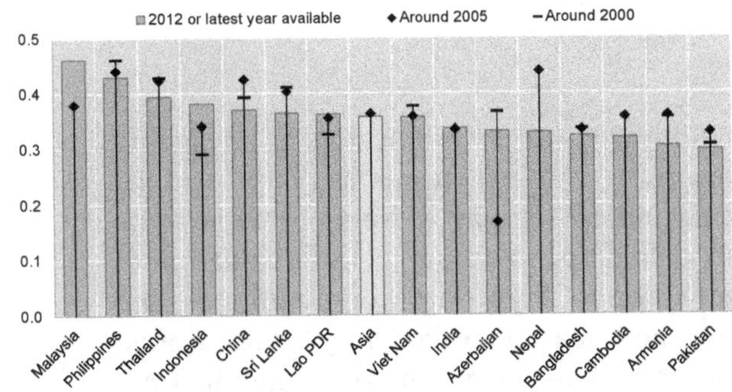

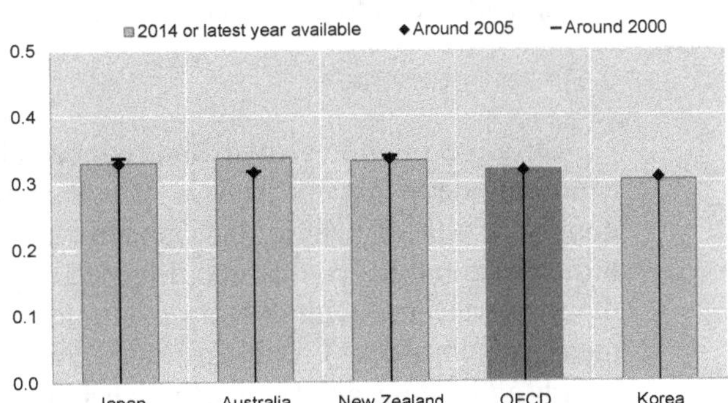

Note: Data for Asian countries and for the OECD are not based on the same definition and therefore not comparable. OECD measures of inequality presented here are based on equalised household disposable income (after taxes and transfers). Income is defined as household disposable income in a particular year. It consists of earnings, self-employment and capital income and public cash transfers; income taxes and social security contributions paid by households are deducted. The income of the household is attributed to each of its members, with an adjustment to reflect differences in needs for households of different sizes. Income inequality among individuals is measured by the Gini coefficient, which is based on the comparison of cumulative proportions of the population against cumulative proportions of income they receive, and it ranges between 0 in the case of perfect equality and 1 in the case of perfect inequality.

For non-OECD member economies in the Asian region, where most people are self-employed in agriculture or casual labourers, income data is often not relevant or non-existent. For most countries, inequality measures are expenditure-based. Expenditure-based measures typically show lower inequality than do income-based measures.

Source: Panel A: World Bank, World Development Indicators, http://databank.worldbank.org/data/reports.aspx?source=world-development-indicators, as in August 2015. Panel B: *OECD Income Distribution Database* (IDD), http://www.oecd.org/social/income-distribution-database.htm.

StatLink ᔆᓵ *http://dx.doi.org/10.1787/888933457280*

By contrast, income inequality in Indonesia increased since 2000 (Figure 1.5). In their study of economic growth, poverty and inequality in Indonesia from 2001 to 2010, Miranti et al. (2013) show that in general, absolute poverty rates have continued to decline but that consumption inequality increased. In part, this outcome is related to the Indonesian tax/benefit system not being very effective at redistributing resources across the population, and targeting support at the poor. At less than 1% of GDP, public social spending on other than pensions and health supports in Indonesia is low: about 33 to 50% of what other large middle income countries, such as Brazil, China India and South Africa, spend in this regard (OECD, 2014a). Further in-kind support such as on education and universal health care (Chapter 2) should be part of a more effective redistribution and integrated anti-poverty policy that works across different levels of government.

Growing income inequality has a negative effect on growth. For example, the rise of income inequality between 1985 and 2005 is estimated to have knocked 4.7 percentage points off cumulative growth between 1990 and 2010, on average across OECD countries for which long time series are available (OECD, 2015b). A key transmission mechanism between inequality and growth is human-capital investment: by hindering human capital accumulation income inequality undermines education opportunities for disadvantaged individuals, lowering social mobility and hampering skills development. It is not just poverty or the incomes of the lowest 10% of the population that inhibit growth: across the OECD, there is a growing gap between lower income households – the bottom 40% of the distribution – and the rest of the population (Cingano, 2014; OECD, 2014b). Anti-poverty programmes will not be enough. Public strategies in many OECD countries need to increase access to public services, such as high-quality education, training and health care, and ensure long-term social investment to create greater equality of opportunities in the long run.

1.3. Life satisfaction

Strong economic growth and reduced absolute poverty are clear indicators of advancing economic development in Asia. It is hard to measure to what extent this has improved the quality of life of people, but subjective well-being indicators may serve to provide some indication on this. To that end, Figure 1.6 presents data on people's subjective evaluation of their satisfaction with life as a whole (see the notes to Figure 1.6 for definitions and measurement issues). Life satisfaction as measured here may be affected by issues around health and living conditions (which have been improving in many an Asian country) but also (family) relationships.

On average across Asia and the OECD, life satisfaction has not changed markedly since the beginning of the crisis (Figure 1.6, Panel B). Life satisfaction increased in about two-thirds of the countries since 2006/08, and the increase appeared most pronounced in Thailand and Azerbaijan. However, except for Japan, life satisfaction has further declined in those countries where it was already low: as, for example, in India and Lao PDR.

People in wealthy countries tend to be more satisfied with life than those in less wealthy countries. On a scale of 1 to 10, life satisfaction scores are slightly more than 1 point higher on average across the OECD than across the Asia region (Figure 1.6). Thais appear to have a higher life satisfaction than what might have been expected on the basis of their average income, but, results for Australia, New Zealand and Singapore on the one hand (averaging at a score of 7 out of 10 in terms of reported life satisfaction), and countries such as Bangladesh, Cambodia, Myanmar and Nepal on the other (Figure 1.6), clearly illustrate the relationship between average life satisfaction and prosperity.

Figure 1.6. Life satisfaction is higher in wealthier countries, but has increased in the majority of Asian countries

Life satisfaction as reported by survey respondents

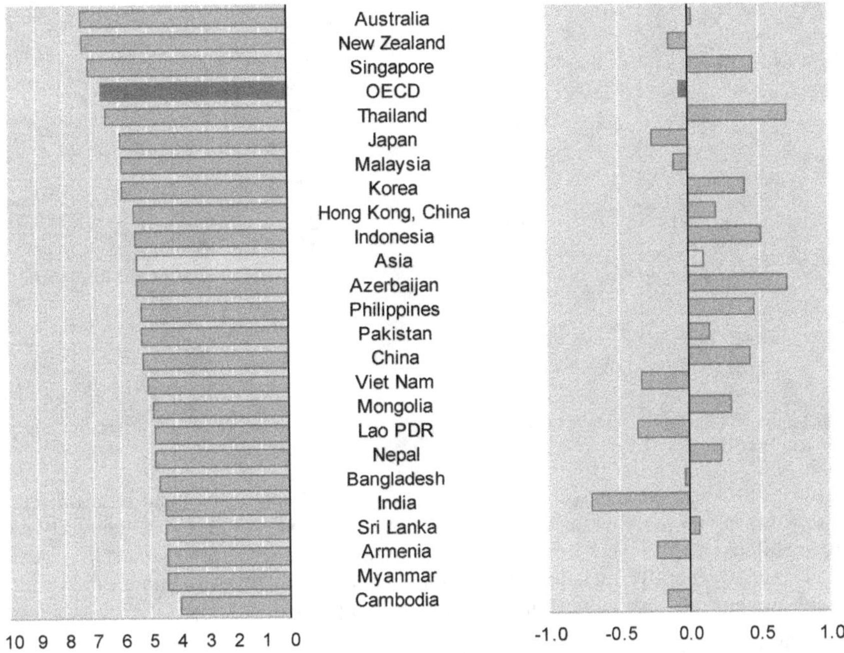

Note: The Gallup World Poll asked respondents to: "Imagine an 11-step ladder where the bottom (0) represents the worst possible life for you and the top (10) represents the best possible life for you. On which step of the ladder do you feel you personally stand at the present time?". The main indicator used in this section is the average country score.

Source: The Gallup World Poll, which is conducted in more than 150 countries around the world based on a common questionnaire Samples are probability based and nationally representative of the resident population aged 15 years and over in a country, including rural areas. Sample sizes vary across countries from 1 000 to 4 000 and results may be affected by sampling and non-sampling error, and variation in response rates. Hence, results should be interpreted with care. To minimise the effect of annual fluctuations in responses related to small sample sizes, results are averaged over a three-year period, or two-year period in case of missing data. If only one observation in a three-year period is available this finding is not reported.

StatLink *http://dx.doi.org/10.1787/888933457293*

1.4.   Asia is coming of age

Women in Asian countries are having fewer children

Birth rates in Asia declined further over the last decade: total fertility rates (TFR – see the note to Figure 1.7) in Asia decreased from 2.6 children per women in 2000 to 2.2 in 2014. Nevertheless, birth rates in Asia remain above the OECD average (Figure 1.7). TFRs declined in two-thirds of these countries declined over the past decade. Countries with high birth rates in 2000 were among the countries that experienced the largest declines in TFRs: Nepal had the largest decrease in the TFR by 1.8 children per women (from 4.0 in 2000 to 2.2 in 2014), followed by Lao PDR (1.3), Cambodia (1.2), Pakistan (1.0) and Bangladesh (1.0). Nevertheless, in all these countries, TFRs remain well above the replacement level of 2.1 children per women in 2014 (see note to Figure 1.7).

Figure 1.7. Fewer children in Asia but Asians can expect to live longer

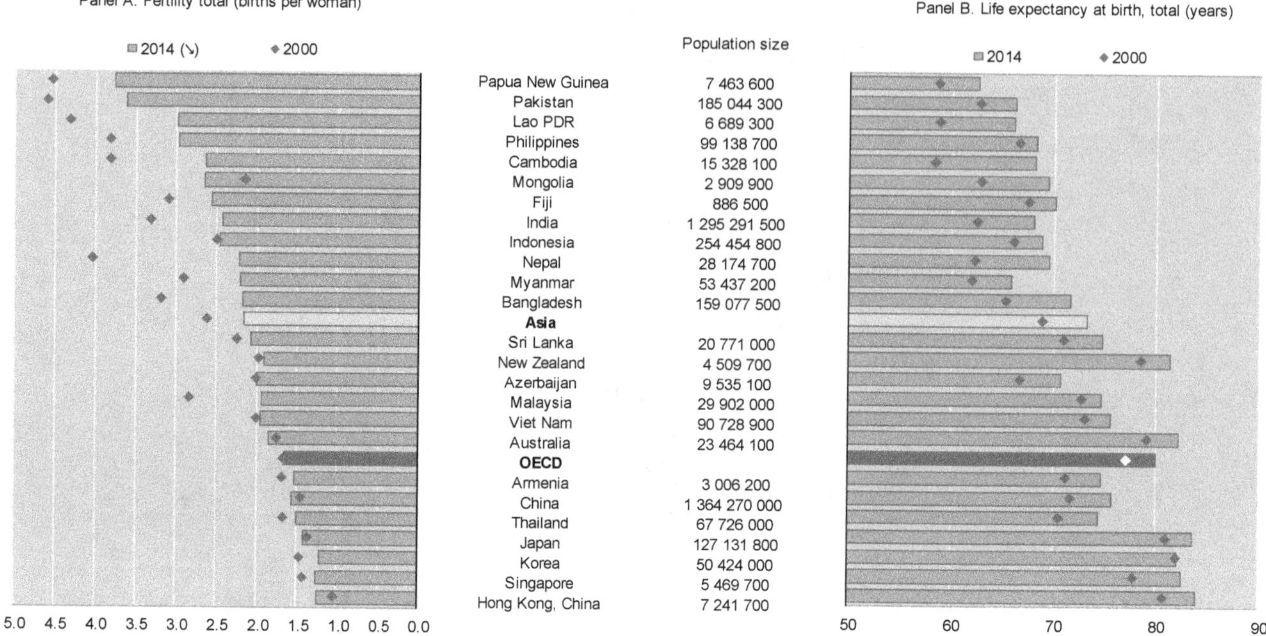

Note: The total fertility rate (TFR) reflects the average number of children born per woman over a lifetime given current age-specific fertility rates and assuming no female mortality during reproductive years. TFRs are generally computed as the sum of age-specific fertility rates defined over five-year intervals. Assuming no migration and that mortality rates remain unchanged, a TFR of 2.1 children per woman is generally sufficient to generate a stable population within a given country – a TFR above or below this "population replacement rate" is likely to produce population growth and population decline, respectively.

Source: World Bank, World Development Indicators, http://databank.worldbank.org/data/reports.aspx?source=world-development-indicators, as in October 2016.

StatLink ᴍꜱᴾ http://dx.doi.org/10.1787/888933457306

Among the countries with TFRs below the OECD average of 1.7 children per women, trends in birth rates are mixed. In Korea, Singapore and Thailand, TFRs continued to fall after 2000 with TFRs in 2014 in Korea (Box 1.2) and Singapore at below 1.3 children per woman. Over the same period TFRs in Hong Kong (China) and Japan increased by less than 0.1 children per women while an anticipation of the recent relaxation of the rules on the number of children per family in China may have contributed to an increase in the TFR from 1.45 in 2000 to 1.56 children per woman in 2014.

Box 1.2. Expanding childcare supports in Korea

There are many different reasons why governments pursue family policy, including combating child poverty, enhancing child development, promote gender equality, mobilise female labour supply and promote economic growth (Adema, 2012). All these factors will have played a role in the formulation of family policy development in Korea, but concern about the persistently low fertility rates is the overriding issue in Korean family policy development. The total fertility rate (TFR) in Korea was 4.5 children per women in 1970, which fell rapidly to 2.07 in 1983 and reached its low point in 2005 at 1.08 children per women. Over the years the Korean Government has developed various initiatives to help parents have as many children as they would like at the time of their choosing. In the early 2000s public policy acknowledged that the government must play an important role in supporting formal childcare to help parents find a better balance between work and family commitments.

Box 1.2. Expanding childcare supports in Korea *(cont.)*

Since the early 2000s, the Korean Government – regardless of the political party in power – has invested heavily in formal childcare by increasing the childcare subsidy and developing other measures that help parents reconcile their work and family responsibilities (see Box 1.4). Since 2000, public spending on early childhood education and care (ECEC) in Korea increased from 0.1% of GDP in 2000 to 0.9% in 2014 (Figure 1.8). Over this period, no other OECD country increased its public investment in ECEC as much as Korea, which is now above the OECD average. Countries where public investment exceeded 1% of GDP in 2014 include (in ascending order) New Zealand, Norway, France, Denmark, Sweden and Iceland. The increase in public investment contributed to an increase in the enrolment rate of children age 0-2 from 4% in 2002 to 36% in 2014 (Statistics Korea) and that of children age 3-5 increased from 31% in 2005 to 92% in 2014 (*OECD Education Database*).

Figure 1.8. Since 2000, Korea increased its public investment in ECEC services almost tenfold

Public expenditure on early childhood education and care as a % of GDP, 2000 and 2013/14 where available

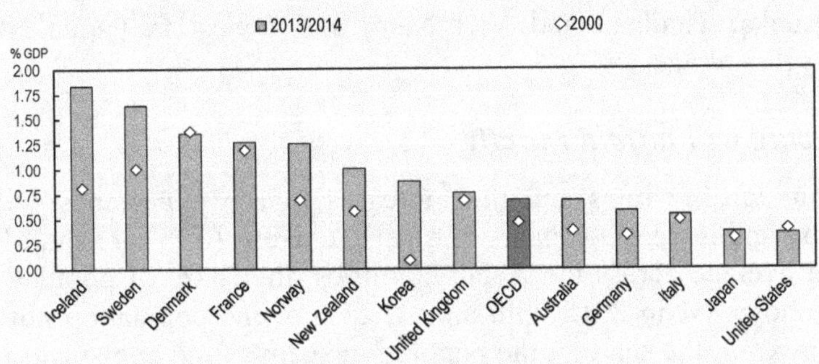

Note: Local governments frequently play a key role in financing and providing childcare services. Such spending is comprehensively recorded in Nordic countries, but in some other (often federal) countries, e.g. the United States it may not be fully captured.

Source: OECD Social Expenditure Database, www.oecd.org/social/expenditure.htm.

StatLink http://dx.doi.org/10.1787/888933457316

The rapid growth of ECEC provision in Korea almost entirely concerns centre-based collective care arrangements. Their development was largely driven by expanding the childcare subsidy to parents who use centre-based childcare (the government pays the subsidy amount on behalf of the parents to the ECEC childcare centre at hand). Korea has long had a childcare subsidy for children from very low-income households, but from 2004 onwards, the income criteria for the subsidy were loosened while the payment rate of the childcare subsidy was increased. In 2013, the income test was scrapped altogether, effectively creating a universal programme of public assistance for centre-based care (Suh and Lee, 2014).

Also, in 2007 the government introduced a subsidised "personal care service", offering parents the option of individual childcare at home. The personal care service is generally a part-time provision, but a full-time service for children age 0-2 years old is available. Service fees and hours are set by government and, parents can receive an allowance towards relevant fees depending on household income. Public budgets for this type of service are relatively limited and the service is used by be less than 1% of children in 2015 (Ministry of Gender Equality and Family Affairs, 2016).

As public investment in childcare services expanded, there was increased debate on the desirability to also support parents who do not use formal childcare services. As a result, in July 2009, the Child Allowance for Home care was introduced for the households with children under 6 who do not use childcare facilities or kindergartens. At introduction, the benefit was limited to very low-income households with children not yet 2 years of age, and was expanded to children age 2 in 2011. However, in 2013, the income-test was abolished and coverage of support was extended to children age 3-5 years. All households with children under 6 became eligible for financial support regardless of their income level: KRW 200 000 (USD 178) for children under 12 months, and KRW 150 000 (USD 135) for children age 1 and KRW 100 000 (USD 90) for children age 2-6 (the allowance is payable until December of the year in which the child becomes 6 years old as the child starts elementary school in March the following year). In 2014, 62% of children age 0-2 (about 840 000 children) received this allowance (MOHW, 2015).

Life expectancy is increasing in Asia

Increases in average life expectancy across Asia (Figure 1.7) to a large extend reflect increases in living standards, better nutrition, water and sanitation, and greater access to better education and health services. Over the past decade, life expectancy at birth increased in all Asian countries by four years from 69 to 73 years on average in 2014. Cambodia recorded the highest increase by 9.9 years, followed by Lao PDR (6.6) and Nepal (6.4). Even from an already high base in 2000, OECD countries in the region recorded an increase in life expectancy: Korea (5.6 years), Australia (3.0), New Zealand (2.8), and Japan (2.3).

As a result and despite the catch-up, life expectancy at birth in all non-OECD Asian countries remained below that in the four OECD countries in the region as well as Hong Kong (China) and Singapore, where on average people can expect to live into their 80s. In 2014, average life expectancy at birth was around the mid-1970s for people China, Malaysia, Sri Lanka, Thailand and Viet Nam, and lowest in Papua New Guinea and Myanmar at 65 years of age.

Population ageing will unfold rapidly

The declining fertility rates and the increases in life expectancy will lead to rapid population ageing and increasing shares of elderly citizens (65 years and older) in societies (Figure 1.9). On average across the Asian countries, the share of population aged 65 and above was just above 8% in 2015 with almost 25% of the population not yet 15 years of age. In Japan, however, the share of the population aged 65 and above was just over 26% in 2015, the highest in the region, while the share of the population under 15 was just below 13 %, the lowest except for Hong Kong (China).

In 2015, Asian countries were relatively young with on average 10.4 persons of working age for each person over 65. In other words, in 2015 at 10.4, the old-age support ratio in Asia was more than twice as high as across the OECD on average (at 4.3). Papua New Guinea is the youngest country with an old-age support ratio of close to 20 followed by Mongolia, Lao PDR and Cambodia (all with an old-age support ratio of around 16). OECD countries in this region are much older and had low old-age support ratios in 2015: Korea (5.6), Australia and New Zealand (4.4), Japan (2.3).

However, Asia is expected to age rapidly in the near future. The old-age support ratio in Asia is projected to decrease by more than one-third from 10.4 to 6.6 by 2030. The old-age support ratio in 2030 is expected to be about half (or less) of what it was in 2015 in Armenia, Azerbaijan, China, Hong Kong (China), Korea, Mongolia, Singapore, Thailand and Viet Nam. Across the OECD on average the old-age support ratio is projected to fall to 2.9 by 2030. By that time Japan (Box 1.3), is projected to have an old-age support ratios which implies that the number of people of working age is less than twice as high as the number of senior citizens (United Nations, 2016).

Figure 1.9. Asia is young but is expected to age considerably over the next 15 years

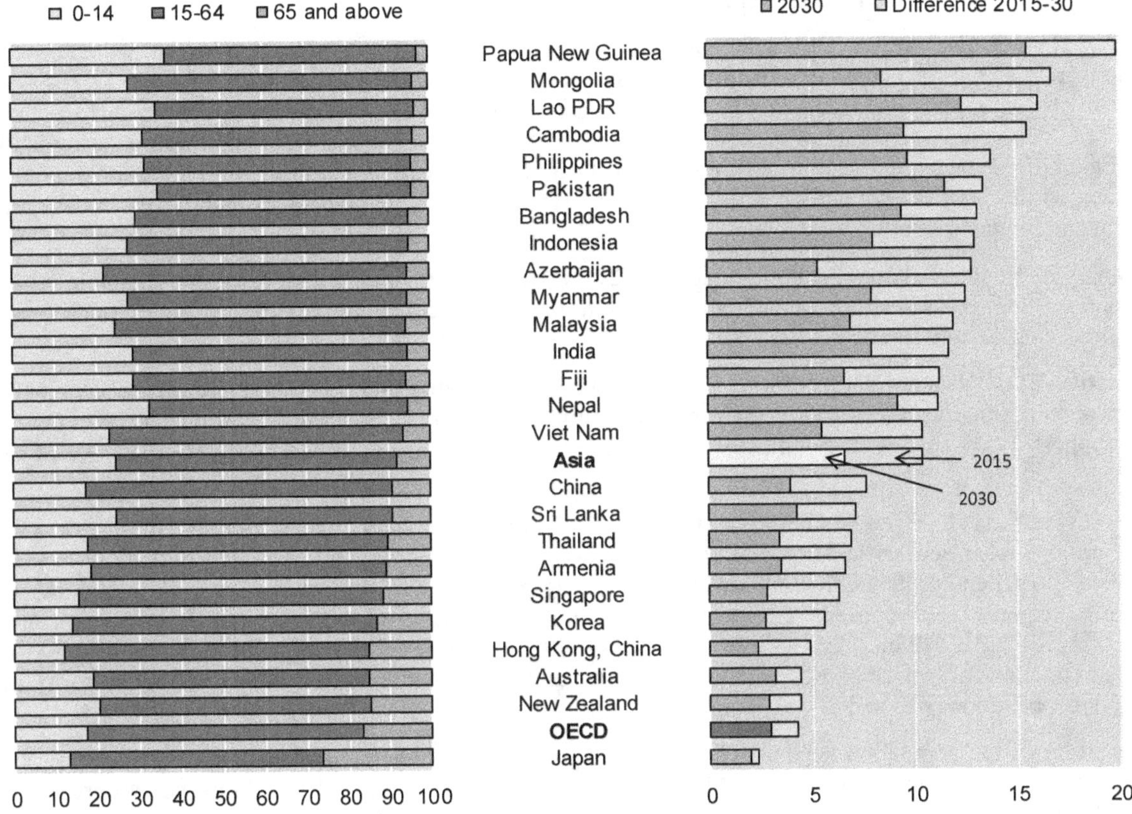

Note: The "old-age support ratio" relates the number of individuals aged 15 to 64 (working age) to the population aged 65 and over (those of "pension age"). All ratios are presented as the number of working age (15-64) people per one non-active person. The old age support ratio thus provides a rough indicator of the number of active people who potentially are economically and socially supporting elderly people.

Source: United Nations, Department of Economic and Social Affairs, Population Division (2015), *World Population Prospects: The 2015 Revision*, data accessed via http://esa.un.org/unpd/wpp/website.

StatLink *http://dx.doi.org/10.1787/888933457320*

Box 1.3. Long-term care insurance in Japan

Long-term care insurance (LTCI) was introduced in Japan in 2000 as a mandatory, contributory-based universal system for the elderly. Until then elderly care services were provided under the Act on Social Welfare for the Elderly that was adopted in 1963. The legislation reflected the "ability-to-pay" principle so that co-payments were relatively high for middle- and high-income households. With population ageing and a change in norms regarding the caring for elderly parents (in-law) living in with working-age families (Campbell and Ikegami, 2000), the number of hospitalised elderly in long-term care rapidly increased. This trends was given further impetus, as from 1973 to 1982 health care to the elderly aged 70 and over was provided for free and the co-payment rates which were re-introduced in 1983 were relatively low.

Box 1.3. Long-term care insurance in Japan *(cont.)*

The number of LTCI recipients increased from 1.49 million in 2000 to 5.11 million in 2015 (MHLW, 2016). The ratio of support recipients increases with age; from less than 5% of those aged 75 and below, to over 60% of those aged 85 and above. However, with population ageing the number of elderly will increase rapidly and challenge the financially sustainability of the LTCI system.

OECD (2011) categorises the Japanese LTCI system as a public long-term care insurance model, which covers large population groups (over a certain age) and which is separately funded from health insurance. LTCI services are available to all senior citizens (aged 65 and over) and those in the 40 to 64 year age group who suffer from geriatric diseases (e.g. dementia) and terminal cancer. Basically, the mandatory contribution is paid by persons aged 40 and over and the retired population in receipt of a pension. Japan does not provide cash benefits for people who provide family care, as the provision of such benefits was considered to mainly perpetuate women's role in care provision (Campbell and Ikegami, 2000).

The Ministry of Health, Labour and Welfare supervises the LTCI system and sets rules on, for example, assessment criteria and service fees. However, municipalities operate the system collecting contributions, assessing care needs, manage funds and pay providers.

A prospective LTCI claimant applies for services at his/her municipality and a local government officer will assess the claim upon a home visit. A local LTCI committee comprised off medical experts will decide upon the required level of support. Local care manager will then draw up a personal care plan, which involves a package of care and support.

Total revenue of the LTCI was JPY 9.6 trillion (USD 92 billion) in 2014, except service fees, JPY 4.9 trillion (USD 47 billion) from general taxation and JPY 4.5 trillion (USD 43 billion) through contributions (NIPSSR2016). This reflects the general principle that 10% of the cost should be covered by the service fee, with the financing of the remainder is equally split between general taxation and mandatory contributions. LTCI benefit spending has increased from JPY 3.3 trillion (USD 31 billion) in 2000 to 9.1 trillion in 2014 (USD 87 billion, equivalent to 2% of GDP, 8% of total social spending). Financial sustainability of the LTCI system has been a key concern for some time: since 2000, contribution rates and co-payments have increased while service coverage has been curtailed.

The proportion of the population aged 75 will increase rapidly and LTCI spending is expected to double between 2015 and 2025 to JPY 20 trillion (or 3.2% of GDP) in 2025 (MHLW,2012). 2011 reform purports a greater reliance on integrated community care (ICC) as the vehicle for long-term care service delivery as such services are less costly than facility or hospital care. ICC is a community-based system that provides various services including health care, long-term care, prevention, housing and livelihood support within the daily living environment, and involves collaboration with medical facilities, promoting prevention, ensuring advocacy and livelihood support services such as a meals provision service and assistance at home (MHLW, 2016). Local governments are co-ordinating all the related programmes to ensure that people living in their community independently as long as possible (NIPSSR, 2014).

1.5.   Education, student skills

In most Asian countries the period of schooling has increased

The level of education of the population gives an indication of its stock of human capital. The average number of years spent in education among the working-age population is the most readily available and cross-nationally comparable measure on educational attainment. The average number of years of schooling in the Asia is 8.3 years, 3.2 years shorter than the OECD average. The "educational attainment gap" in Asia is so large because: 1) in some of the Asian countries considered here – Pakistan, Bangladesh, Lao PDR, Papua New Guinea and Nepal – the average period of schooling is very low; and 2) at close to 12 years of schooling on average, working-age populations in the Asian OECD countries have the highest level of educational attainment in the region (Figure 1.10).

The educational attainment gap between Asia and the OECD has changed little over the past ten years as the average increase in the numbers of years of schooling across the two areas was around one year over the 1990-2013 period (OECD, 2014c, includes trends since 1990). There has been catch-up in terms of educational attainment in some Asian countries, in Pakistan from a very low base, but also in Malaysia, Singapore, Viet Nam and Hong Kong (China) (Figure 1.10).

Figure 1.10. Educational attainment is increasing in Asia

Education attainment in years of schooling

Panel A. Average years of total schooling, 2014

Panel B. Change in average years of total schooling 2000-2014 (in years)

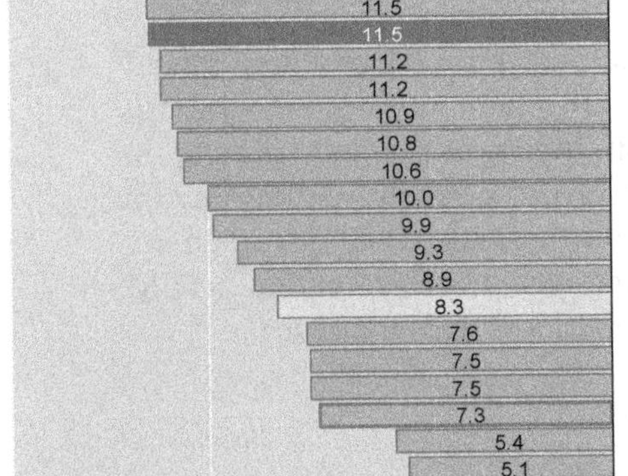

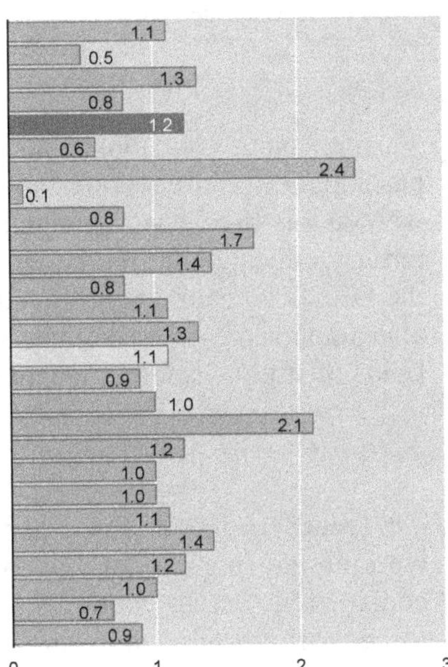

Source: UNDP, International Human Development Indicators from: http://hdr.undp.org.

StatLink ⊡ *http://dx.doi.org/10.1787/888933457338*

Some Asian countries were in the group of top-performing countries in the OECD Programme for International Student Assessment – OECD PISA survey, which evaluates the knowledge and skills of the world's 15-year-olds. Students from Singapore and Hong Kong (China) did particularly well as they had the highest average PISA test scores in both mathematics and reading literacy (Figure 1.11). At the other end of the spectrum students in Indonesia, Kazakhstan, Malaysia and Thailand scored below the Asian and OECD averages.

OECD PISA results, a benchmark of student performance worldwide, can be taken to reflect the increasing skills of many students in Asia and the scope of rising productivity and competitiveness in future. However, as shown in the total schooling years above, access to junior high and high school level education is still an issue in many Asian countries and for many Asian students.

Figure 1.11. Some Asian countries outperform OECD countries in OECD PISA surveys

Student Literacy level of mathematics and reading, 2015

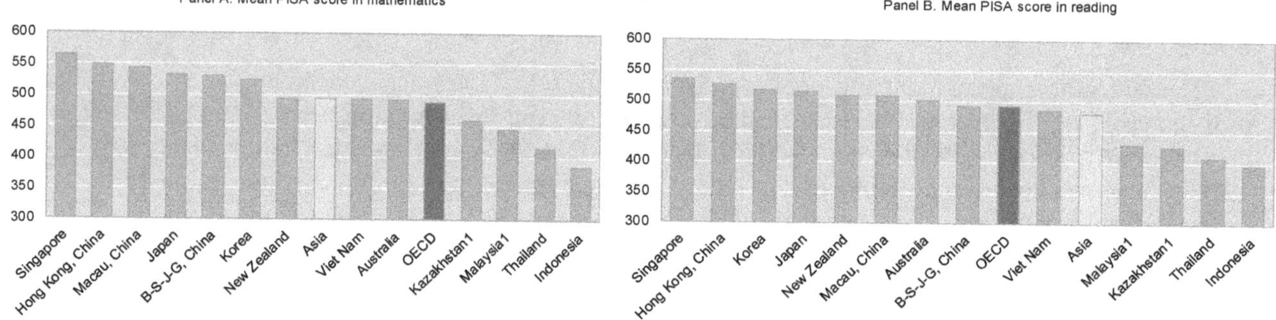

BSJG is an acronym for Beijing, Shanghai, Jiangsu and Guangdong.

1. Kazakhstan and Malaysia: coverage is too small to ensure comparability

Source: OECD PISA assessment 2015 (http://www.oecd.org/pisa/).

StatLink *http://dx.doi.org/10.1787/888933457344*

Increasing educational attainment enlarges the potential for productive employment participation and economic growth. In particular, educational attainment among (young) women has risen fast although across the Asia/Pacific region there remains a gender gap in tertiary educational attainment of four percentage points in favour of men – unlike across the OECD where there is a gender gap in favour of women. Furthermore, young women are also underrepresented among students and graduates of degrees in the so-called STEM fields of study – science, technology, engineering and mathematics (OECD, 2014c).

1.6. Labour force participation and employment

Trends in labour force participation – which measures the proportion of a country's working-age population 15 years and over either in work or looking for work – varied considerably across countries in Asia over the past ten years. Both male and female labour force participation rates increased in Mongolia, Viet Nam as well as Armenia and Azerbaijan which reflects a general trend across Central and Western Asia. In most Asian countries male labour force participation rates edged down over the 2005-15 period, while the number of countries where female participation fell almost equals the number of countries where female labour force participation increased (Figure 1.12).

Across Asia, cross-national variation in employment rates is similar to that in labour force participation rates across (Table 1.A1.1 in Annex 1.A1). Overall, however it appears that employment to population rates have edged down suggesting that despite large job creation – 21 million net new jobs alone in 2015 (ILO, 2016a), the population of working age has grown even faster over the past ten years.

In terms of employment status, wage and salary employment is growing in Asia, but still only accounts for less than half of total employment – 43.5% in 2015 compared to 34.8% in 2005 (ILO, 2015a). Changes in the share of "own-account workers" and "self-employed with employees" have been limited but here has been an important decline – by 10 percentage points – in the share of contributing family workers (from 21.3% in 2005 to 11.3% in 2015 on average in Asia). These shifts have been most pronounced for workers in China and Mongolia as well as Cambodia, Lao PDR and Myanmar (ILO, 2015a).

The move towards the production of higher value added products is typically associated with higher income. This increase have to some extent trickled down to workers at the lower end of income distribution in Asia (ILO, 2016a), which has contributed to a reduction of the incidence of working poverty, when considered against an absolute poverty benchmark. Over the 2005-15 period, the share of workers living in poverty – i.e. those living on less than USD PPP 2 – declined from 30 to 10% in East Asia, from 45 to 22.5% in South-East Asia, but despite a significant decline remains high at over 50% in South Asia (ILO, 2016a).

Gender gaps in employment

Labour force participation rates are generally lower for women than for men and gender participation gaps are most significant in South Asian countries: Figure 1.12 shows that in 2015, the largest gender gaps in labour force participation were recorded for Pakistan, India and Sri Lanka. Women in these countries often face considerable educational, cultural and institutional barriers to labour market participation.

Female labour force participation actually declined over the 2005-15 period in 11 out the 25 countries for which data are presented here, and nowhere more so than in India where female labour force participation fell by around 10 percentage points to just over a quarter in 2015 (Figure 1.12). India is committed to reducing the gender gap in labour force participation by 25% by 2025 (OECD et al., 2014), which as Agenor, Mares and Sorsa (2015) showed could boost the growth rate by 2 percentage points over time. Similarly, the ADB and ILO estimated that women's limited access to employment causes a loss in economic growth to the Asia/Pacific region of around USD 42 to 47 billion per annum (ADB and ILO, 2011). To realise women's economic potential it is important to enforce the existing gender equality legislation and develop infrastructure (e.g. transport) and other labour market supports.

Figure 1.12. There is no clear trend in labour force participation in Asia, but gender gaps are often large

Labour force participation rates, by gender, 2005 2015, age group 15 and over

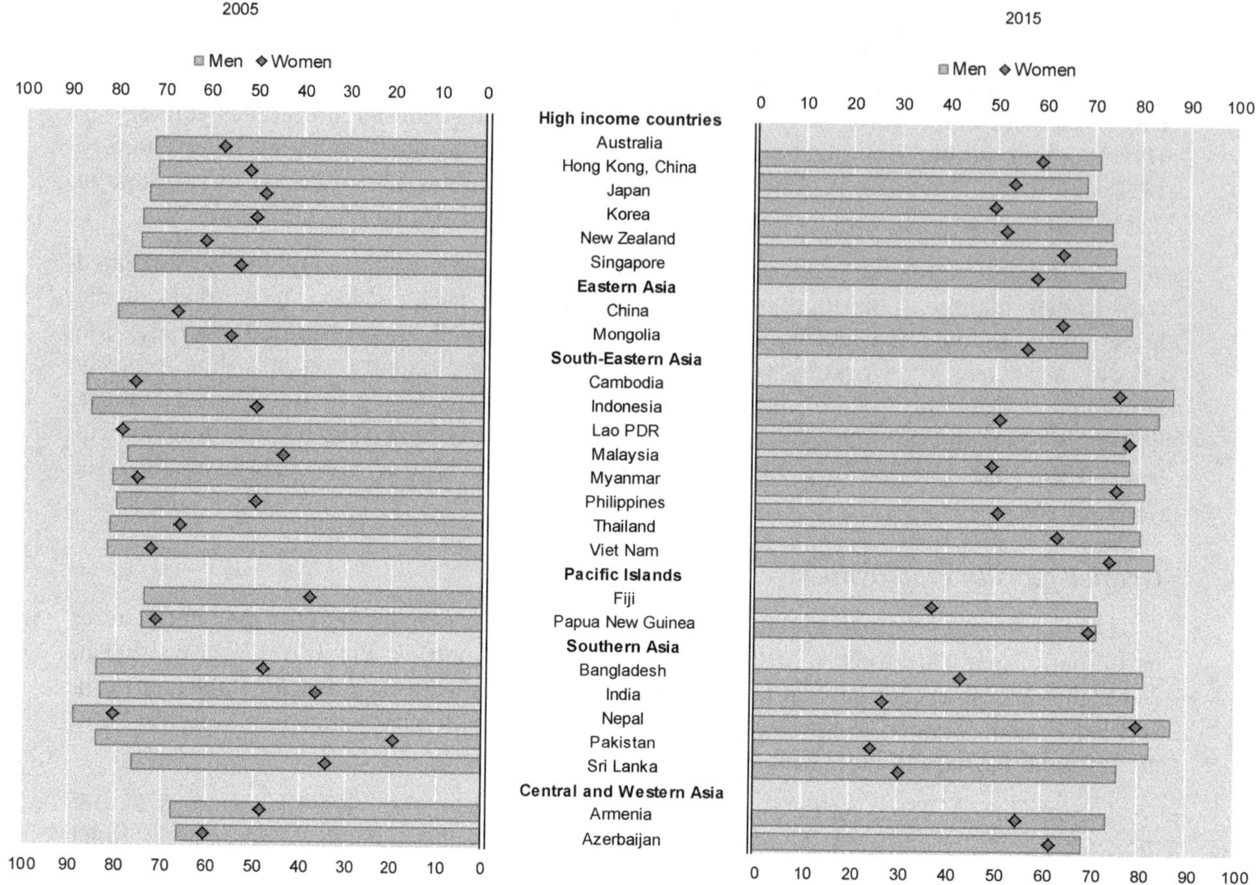

Source: ILO, Trends Econometric Models, October 2015; ILO Research Department, OECD Labour Force Statistics for OECD countries.

StatLink ⌗ http://dx.doi.org/10.1787/888933457351

In India, labour force participation is higher among the poor and declines with education and family incomes. This goes against the trend in most countries and reflects a range of factors, including social norms as staying at home which is frequently considered to increase the family's social status (OECD, 2014d). Social and cultural factors are key driving forces of keeping women outside the labour force, especially in Northern India (Sorsa et al., 2015). Many laws provide for gender equality, however, they are often not implemented in practice, and in terms of discrimination, India scores high in the OECD Development Centre Social Institutions and Gender Indicator (SIGI), which measures the impact of laws and socioeconomic factors on women's status (OECD Development Centre, 2014a). Women are disadvantaged by inheritance laws which restrict financial independence, access to credit and independent decision making while labour laws restrict women's working hours and access to certain occupations (OECD, 2014d).

China is the other populous Asian country where female employment rates have fallen. With economic restructuring female employment rates started to decline in the mid-1990s and by 2015 around two-thirds of women over 15 were in paid work. Increased partner earnings, a lack of access to paid maternity leave in the private sector and affordable quality early childhood education and care (ECEC) supports have contributed to the decline in female employment participation (Shin et al., 2013).

Mothers may be the main users of child-related leave provisions, but among OECD countries there is growing debate on leave arrangements that target or are available only to fathers (Adema et al., 2015). As well as affording fathers the opportunity to support mother and child directly after childbirth, father-specific leaves are likely to encourage them to engage in parenting and, to some degree at least, promote male unpaid work within the household. Moreover, father-specific leave is likely to reduce grounds for leave-associated employer discrimination against female employees: as long as mothers remain the main, almost exclusive, users of leave, there is a risk that employers will be less likely to hire young women on permanent or regular employment contracts and investing less in their career opportunities and training than in men's (see also OECD, 2012). That risk would be reduced if large numbers of young fathers would take up child-related leave not just for one or two days, but for months at a time. Furthermore, the evidence from across the OECD suggests that the provision of father-specific leave may also affect fathers' involvement in parenting and/or housework, their working hours, their own well-being, and the well-being of their children (OECD, 2016a and 2016b).

Family and gender policy in Japan and Korea is geared towards helping both parents to stay in work and have as many children as they would like to at the time of their choosing. For that reason, public policy in both these Asian countries provides for one year of paid leave for both parents as an individual entitlement. In this sense, Korea and Japan are leaders in parental leave policies for fathers, not just in Asia, but across the OECD (Figure 1.13).

Figure 1.13. Korea and Japan provide eligible fathers with an individual entitlement of paid leave for a year

Duration of paid leave reserved for fathers (paid paternity leave and/or father-specific parental leave) in weeks, 2015

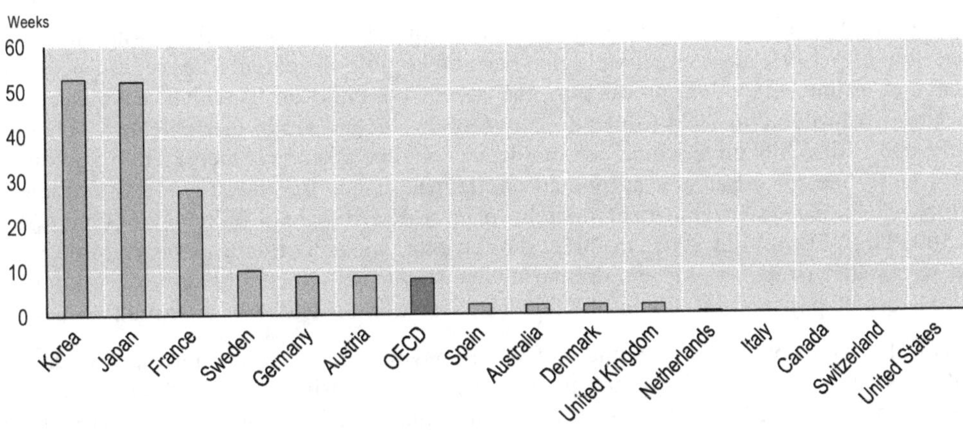

Note: Information refers to entitlements to paternity leave, "father quotas" or periods of parental leave that can be used only by the father and cannot be transferred to the mother, and any weeks of sharable leave that must be taken by the father or second parent in order for the family to qualify for "bonus" weeks of parental leave. Information as of April 2015.

Source: OECD Family Database.

StatLink *http://dx.doi.org/10.1787/888933457365*

In Korea, parents have to take leave parental leave sequentially (Box 1.4), In Japan, both parents also have an individual entitlement of one year of paid leave, they have to use this before the child's first birthday – or until the child turns 15 months old if both parents take some leave. Nordic countries often have "mummy and daddy quotas", or specific portions of the overall parental leave period that are reserved exclusively for mothers or fathers. Iceland and, since 1 January 2016, Sweden reserve 12 weeks for both parents. Other countries offer "bonus periods", where a couple may qualify for some extra weeks of paid leave if both parents use a certain period of leave. Germany, for example, provides two months of additional parental leave payments if both parents claim the parental leave allowance for at least two months.

Box 1.4. Child-related leave supporting parents with very young children in Korea

To help parents with the reconciliation of work and family life when children are young, Korean policy has developed a system of child-related leaves that facilitates the provision of full-time personal parental care to very young children until their second birthday. The Korean system has three types of employment protected child-related leave: maternity, paternity and parental leave (see Kim, 2016 for an overview). Since the early 2000s, the Employment Insurance system provides financial supports for maternity and parental leave, and policy moved to increase the generosity of provisions by increasing payment rates as well as the age of the child up to which parents can use parental leave.

Maternity leave. A period of 60-day maternity leave was introduced in 1953 and since then employers are responsible for continued wage payments to mothers on leave. However, the EI system reimburses employers up to certain limit depending on firm size. In 2001 the leave period was extended to 90 days, and employers are reimbursed by the EI system for 30 days of leave taken up to a ceiling of KRW 1 350 000 (USD 1 209). For workers in small and medium enterprises (SMEs), EI reimburses from 2006 onwards employers for 90 days of leave up to an amount of KRW 4 050 000 (USD 3 627).

Paternity leave. The employer must give three to five days' leave to fathers whose spouses give birth, upon the employee's request. The first three days are fully paid for by the employer since 2012. Leave must be taken within 30 days after child-birth.

Parental leave. An entitlement to unpaid parental leave until the child's first birthday was introduced in 1988 for female employees only. In 1995, male employees also became eligible for parental leave, but only one parent could take parental leave at a time. Since its introduction, the age of the child up to which leave can be taken has also increased: from the first birthday in 1998 to age 8 – entering the second grade in elementary school in 2014. From 2006 onwards, the age of the child up to which parental leave could be taken was increased to the fourth birthday, and one year parental leave became a parent's individual entitlement. Since the introduction of income support during parental leave through the EI system, payment rates have increased from: KRW 200 000 (USD 178) per month in 2001, to KRW 500 000 (USD 448) in 2007. In 2011, the flat-rate payment structure was reformed into an earnings-related payment worth 40% of the employee's ordinary wage (i.e. for contractually agreed working hours regardless of bonuses and/or overtime pay) up to a ceiling of KRW 1 million (almost USD 900) per month.

Take-up of leave. The extension of duration and increase in payment rates have contributed to an expansion in the number of employees taking maternity leave and parental leave in the private sector, the number of workers taking maternity leave increase fivefold from 2002 to 2015 when almost 100 000 mothers took maternity leave (MOEL, 2010, 2016a and 2016b). In 2015, there were about 90,000 employees who took parental leave, which suggest that most mothers who took maternity leave also used parental leave. However, not all non-regular workers are entitled to maternity leave and many mothers still withdraw from the labour force around child birth: in 2015, the share of mothers in the private sector taking maternity leave accounted for 22% of new-born babies.

Male employees taking parental leave accounted for 8.5% of those taking parental leave in 2015 (MOEL, 2017). The number has increased sharply since 2011 (Figure 1.14) when the parental leave allowance changed into an earnings-related payment (see above). The average length of leave taken by fathers in Korea is 8.2 months, compared to 9.8 months for mothers in 2015 (MOEL, 2016b). Clearly, taking fathers have a hard time deciding to take leave, but when they do, they take leave for a considerable period of time.

Box 1.4. Child-related leave supporting parents with very young children in Korea *(cont.)*

Figure 1.14. Percentage of male employees among total employees taking parental leave in Korea

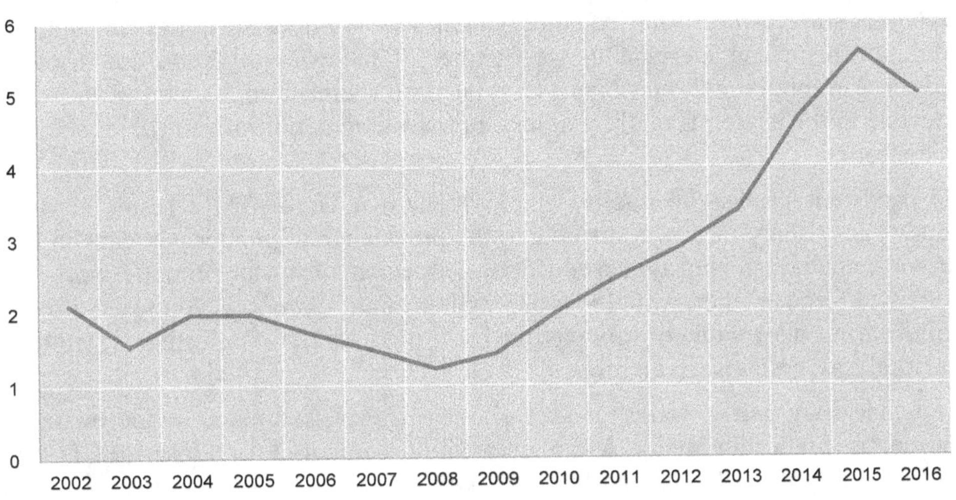

Source: Ministry of Employment and Labour, Korea.

StatLink *http://dx.doi.org/10.1787/888933457370*

In order to encourage fathers to take parental leave after the mothers, the "Daddy's month" was introduced in October 2014: In case one parent (usually the mother) takes parental leave first and the other parent (usually the father) takes parental leave afterwards, the allowance for the first month for the second parent was 100% of the ordinary wage up to a maximum of KRW 1 500 000 (USD 1 350). From 2016, this "daddy's month" was extended to three months. This measure is expected to further increase the use of leave by fathers and is illustrative of Korean's policy drive towards a more equal sharing of leave between parents and increasing father's involvement in caring for children.

Gender gaps in unpaid work

Women are much more likely than men to be involved in unpaid work in and around the house which often involves providing care to children or other family members In OECD countries the gender gap is smallest in Denmark where women "only" spend one hour more per day on unpaid work than men (OECD, 2016c), while the OECD average is 2.5 hours per day (Figure 2.10). In less developed economies, time spent on unpaid work includes care responsibilities, but also time-consuming activities such as looking for fuel or queuing for water. As societal norms frequently dictate that women are mainly responsible for such work, gender gaps in unpaid work can be substantial. Time spent on unpaid household work has been identified as a major contributor to the persisting gender differences in formal labour market outcomes. In Asia the gender gap in unpaid work is about three hours per day, and such gaps are particularly large in Pakistan and India where women spend four to five more hours per day on unpaid work than men (OECD, 2011b). In India, unpaid workers account for a very large proportion of the rural female workforce, and many poor women have the "double duty" of caring for the household as well as engaging in outside employment. Infrastructural developments regarding water, electricity and transport could free up a lot of time women currently spent on unpaid work.

Gender pay gaps

When in paid work women in Asia are more likely than men to experience vulnerable work conditions, often unpaid family work, particularly in low-income countries with low general levels of educational attainment. Family workers account for nearly one in five females employed in Asia, compared to less than 7% of male employment (ILO, 2016a and 2016b). A shift towards salaried employment does not necessarily lessen quality issues. For example, the recent increase in the number of factories in Asian countries such as Bangladesh, Cambodia and Viet Nam, facilitated an increase of women in the workforce and a decline in the share officially workers, but working conditions in these factories are a serious concern.

The persistent barriers to quality employment that women face result in substantial gender pay gaps. Many factors contribute to the prevalence of gender pay gaps in favour of men in Asia, including inadequate education (especially for older female workers); high rates of workforce withdrawal and career interruption among young and prime-age (i.e., childbearing age) women; low-paying jobs; high levels of informality; attitudes and social institutions; and, discrimination.

The gender pay gap in terms of gross hourly wages, estimated at the median of the distribution, is higher in many Asian economies compared to most OECD countries (Figure 1.15). Indonesia, Korea and India all have gender pay gaps that exceed 30% and at over 50% are particularly large in India. On average across the OECD gender pay gaps are 15% with gender pay differences in New Zealand being relatively small at only 7% at the median.

Figure 1.15. Gender pay gaps are substantial in Asia

Difference between female median wage and male median wage divided by the male median wage, 2014

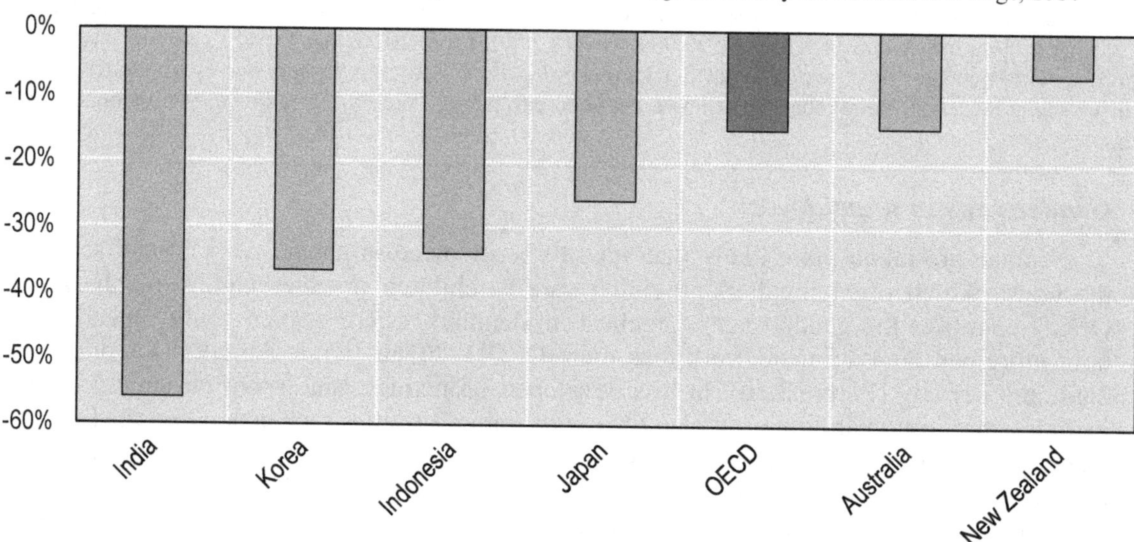

Note: Data refer to 2014 for all countries except for India. They refer to hourly wage for full time employees (working more than 30 hour per week in the main job), except for India for which they refer to weekly earnings of full-time employees and Japan and Korea, for which they refer to monthly wages of full-time employees.

Source: Household, Income and Labour Dynamics for Australia, National labour force survey for Korea, Basic Survey on Wage Structure for Japan, National Sample Survey for India, National Labour Force Survey (Sakernas) for Indonesia, Household Economic Survey for New Zealand.

StatLink ᵃᵉˢᵖ *http://dx.doi.org/10.1787/888933457380*

The OECD job-quality framework and emerging economies

Job quality is an inherently multi-dimensional concept that refers to those job characteristics that contribute to the well-being of workers. Following the influential report by the Stiglitz-Sen-Fitoussi Commission (Stiglitz et al., 2009), which identified eight dimensions of well-being, the OECD Job Quality Framework is structured around three dimensions that are closely related to people's employment situation: earnings quality; labour market security; and, quality of the working environment (OECD, 2014e). The *OECD Employment Outlook* further developed this framework and adapted it to emerging economies in view of the prevailing data limitations and their labour market characteristics, in particular, the weaknesses of their social protection (inadequacy of benefits and/or limited coverage of social insurance schemes), and the high incidence of informality and high incidence of working poverty (OECD, 2015c).

- **Earnings quality.** This dimension of job quality refers to the extent to which employment contributes to the material living standards of workers and their families. The average level of earnings provides a key benchmark for assessing the degree to which having a job ensures good living conditions, while the way earnings are distributed across the workforce also matters greatly for well-being. This approach reflects the growing body of evidence that absolute and relative earnings matter for well-being and that individuals display a certain degree of inequality aversion in their preferences (OECD, 2014e). Furthermore, since emerging economies are characterised by considerably larger earnings inequality than OECD countries, this approach appears to be particularly well suited to assess workers' well-being in these countries.

- **Labour market security.** In OECD countries becoming and remaining unemployed is the most significant labour market risk for a worker. However, while the unemployment risk may also be significant in emerging economies it is of a different nature than in OECD countries as the weakness of social insurance schemes makes unemployment unaffordable and pushes many workers into "last resort jobs" with very low and unpredictable earnings. Hence, under such conditions, a useful complementary measure of labour market risk is the of falling into such undesirable jobs, defined here by working with earnings below a threshold of "extreme low pay" (as translates into a disposable per capita income of USD 2 PPP per day in a typical household containing a single earner who works full-time (Bongaarts, 2001), which suggest absolute material deprivation for those concerned.

Unemployment risks in emerging economies are comparable with the OECD average. However, otherwise, emerging economies fare worse in terms of earnings quality, considerable risks for falling into low pay with little income support by means of social transfers, leading to high overall levels of labour market insecurity, while the high incidence of long working hours suggests that the quality of the working environment is low relative to OECD countries. Furthermore, among the group of emerging economics included in the OECD 2015 analysis Indonesia and India stood out with a high degree of labour market insecurity related to extremely low pay (which concerns at least a quarter of households), and low job quality as proxied by the high incidence (close to 15 of workers) with working hours over 60 hours per week). Available results for China compare better with OECD averages, but these results are based on urban survey-data only (OECD, 2015c).

- The **quality of the working environment** captures non-economic aspects of job quality and includes factors that relate to the nature and content of the work performed, working-time arrangements and workplace relationships. However, for most of the emerging economies, because information on working conditions is often scarce and limited in scope. To overcome these limitations, the quality of the working environment has been proxied by the incidence of very long working hours. This is by no means an ideal indicator as evidence on the relationship between long work hours and life satisfaction is mixed, but otherwise results suggest that working very long hours impairs workers' physical and mental health, particularly when employees have little control on the number of hours they work and/or on their work schedule (Bassanini and Caroli, 2015; OECD, 2011c and 2016d).

Informal employment

One key determinant of job quality is whether or not workers through their employment relationship are covered by social protection arrangements. If workers do not pay social security contributions – either as employee or self-employed workers, and/or their employers do not pay social security contributions on their behalf, these workers are generally regarded to be in informal employment (see the notes to Figure 1.16 for a discussion of relevant concepts), and improving social protection coverage among these workers is a key policy challenges (Box 1.5).

Available evidence confirms that workers in informal employment face higher poverty risks than workers in formal employment – for example, in China and Viet Nam this risk is three times as high (ILO, 2017, *forthcoming*). The elevated poverty risk of workers in informal employment is related to many factors such as the over-representation of younger and older workers and/or workers with low educational attainment. There also is a relatively high incidence of short working hours among workers in informal employment and associated underemployment. For example, in the first quarter of 2016, 14.3% of workers in informal employment in Indonesia worked less than 20 hours a week compared with 4.2% of workers in formal employment, and many of these workers would like to work more hours to strengthen household incomes (ILO, 2017, *forthcoming*).

By its very nature the extent of informal employment is hard to measure, but available estimates suggest that it is widespread in Asia. Figure 1.16 presents estimates on the share of informal employment in total employment, which suggests that informal employment often concerns at least half of all workers. In many countries, including Bangladesh, Cambodian, India, Indonesia, and Pakistan, its scope is much larger and "informality" concerns around 80% of workers. Available estimates on China suggest that informal employment concerns about 20 to 30% of workers in urban areas (ILO, 2013; OECD, 2015c). However, these estimates are likely to underestimate the true extent of informality in China as it does not cover workers in rural areas and the agricultural sector.

Figure 1.16. Informal employment is widespread in Asia

Informal employment in total employment, 2016 or latest year available

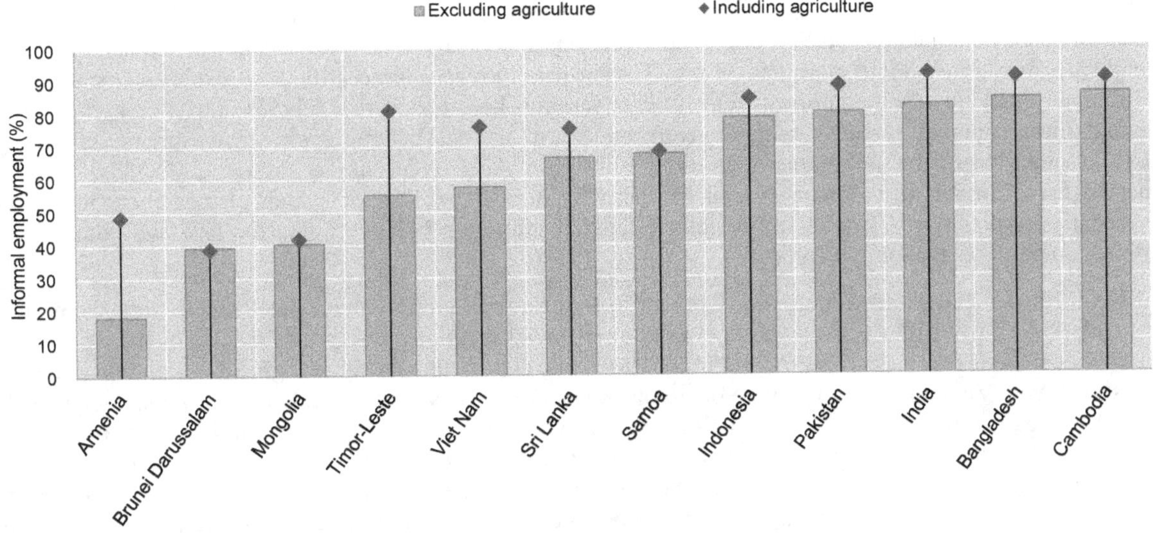

Note: The term "informal economy" encompasses all economic activities by workers or economic units that are – in law or practice – not covered or insufficiently covered by formal arrangements. Jobs are identified as informal according to the characteristics of the employment relationship and status in employment. Informal jobs can occur in the formal sector as well as in the informal sector or in households (e.g. in the case of domestic work). Employees are considered to have informal jobs if their employment relationship is not subject to labour regulation, taxation, social protection or entitlement to certain employment benefits (advance notice of dismissal, paid annual or sick leave, etc.). Own account workers, employers and members of producers' co-operatives are considered to have an informal job if the production unit is informal. All contributing (unpaid) family workers are considered to have informal jobs. Activities of persons engaged in the production of goods for own final users are also considered informal jobs. Informal enterprises are private unincorporated enterprises which are not registered under specific forms of national legislation, such as factories or commercial acts, tax or social security laws, professional groups' regulatory acts, or similar acts, laws or regulations established by national legislative bodies and/or whose employees are not registered. (For a discussion of methodological concepts and measurement issues regarding informal employment, see Hussmanns, 2004; ILO, 2013; and OECD, 2015c.) Data refer to 2012 for Samoa, India and Cambodia, 2013 for Timor-Leste, Sri Lanka and Bangladesh, 2014 for Armenia, Brunei Darussala and Mongolia, 2015 for Pakistan and Viet Nam and 2016 for Indonesia.

Source: ILO ILOSTAT Database (download 19 October 2016).

StatLink *http://dx.doi.org/10.1787/888933457398*

Box 1.5. Extending social insurance coverage among workers in informal employment in Viet Nam

In 2015, following the ILO definition of informal employment, 76.1% of the workers (including agriculture) and 57.7% when excluding agriculture, are in informal employment in Viet Nam (ILO estimates based on the Viet Nam labour force survey 2015.

Extending social protection coverage is an important public policy objective in Viet Nam. The Social Insurance Law passed in June 2006, and most recently amended in 2014, covers public and private employees (in establishments with at least one employee in the event of disability, sickness, maternity, work injury, and old age on a compulsory basis. Amidst the global financial crisis in 2008-09, an unemployment insurance scheme was introduced to replace the existing severance pay system in 2009. Since 2008, workers in informal employment are eligible, on a voluntary basis, for the retirement and survivor pension scheme. However, despite the expansion of social insurance coverage over the past decade, as of November 2015, at most 12 million and 0.23 million workers are respectively covered by the compulsory and voluntary social insurance schemes (VSS, 2015), which accounts for around 20% of the labour force; and 10.2 million workers contribute the unemployment insurance scheme (VSS, 2015).

Box 1.5. Extending social insurance coverage among workers in informal employment in Viet Nam
(cont.)

The coverage remains particularly low among small and medium enterprises and workers with short-term contracts. Intentional evasion from making social security contributions persist by means of non-registration of businesses and/or employees working without contracts, employees who are not registered with the Viet Nam Social Security (VSS) – full non-compliance, and employees registered at earnings below their real salaries (partial non-compliance). Delay and default in payment of social insurance contributions on the part of employers is widespread. According to VSS (2015), social insurance debt amounted to 8 600 billion Viet Nam Dong (about USD 385 000) as per 31 October 2015. Affiliation to voluntary social insurance is limited because of a lack of awareness and a weak financial incentive structure of the scheme (unrealistic lengthy minimum period of contributions and relatively high contributions compared to available incomes).

Aware of the lack of social protection among workers in the informal employment, the Party Central Committee's Resolution No. 15-NQ/TW of 2012 set a target to achieve of social insurance coverage for 50% of the workforce by 2020. To help achieve the target on coverage and increase financial sustainability in light of population ageing and economic slowdown, Vietnam reformed its Social Insurance Law in November 2014. Key adjustments include extending the scope of application of the law to all employees with contracts of at least one month duration, including migrant workers, improving voluntary participation among the self-employed and workers with non-standard employment contracts, clarifying the definition of the reference wage used to calculate contributions, allowing more flexibility to payment schedules, matching voluntary contributions with government subsidies, and strengthening labour and social insurance inspection.

It is as yet an open question as to whether the 2014 reform of the Social Insurance Law that came into effect in January 2016 will translated into de facto increase coverage of social protection among workers. Labour inspection capacity also needs to be strengthened and a system of penalties for non-compliance needs to be put in place and effectively enforced (OECD Development Centre, 2015).

1.7. Concluding remarks

Over the past ten years, the socio-economic context in Asia has changed. Strong economic growth has contributed to a reduction of poverty and greater prosperity has contributed to reduced total fertility rates and increased life expectancy.

Asia is increasing investment in education and its educational attainment is going up, even though there is huge variation in educational attainment and PISA scores among 15-years old students across countries. Asia has to make the most of window of opportunity that an increasingly educated working-age population offers and prepare for the onset of population ageing in years to come. Indeed, population ageing in Asia is expected to unfold rapidly with the number of people of working age (15-65) per senior citizen (65+) projected to fall by over one-third from 10.4 in 2015 to 6.6 by 2030.

While women are catching up with men in terms of educational attainment, labour force participation rates are generally lower for women than for men and gender participation gaps are most significant in South Asian countries. Available evidence on gender pay gaps suggest these are wider in Asia than across the OECD, and can be as high as 50% at the median. Women are more likely to face vulnerable employment conditions, work in informal jobs, and therefore have less access to social protection.

At present many workers work in informal employment, often for long hours at little pay and without social protection coverage. Extending social protection coverage (Chapter 2) and improving the job quality of workers in terms of earnings quality, labour market insecurity and the quality of the work environment will be one of Asia's major challenges in future.

References

ADB (2015), "Asian Development Outlook 2015 Update: Enabling Women, Energizing Asia", Asian Development Bank, Manila, the Philippines.

ADB and ILO (2011), "Women and Labour Markets in Asia: Rebalancing Towards Gender Equality in Labour Markets in Asia", ILO Regional Office for Asia and the Pacific, Bangkok, Asian Development Bank, Manila.

Adema, W. (2012), "Setting the Scene: The Mix of Family Policy Objectives and Packages Across the OECD", *Children and Youth Services Review*, Vol. 34, pp. 487–498.

Adema, W., C. Clarke and V. Frey (2015), "Paid Parental Leave: Lessons from OECD Countries and Selected U.S. States", *OECD Social, Employment and Migration Working Papers*, No. 172, OECD Publishing, Paris, http://dx.doi.org/10.1787/5jrqgvqqb4vb-en.

Agénor, P., J. Mares and P. Sorsa (2015), "Gender Equality and Economic Growth in India: A Quantitative Framework", *OECD Economics Department Working Papers*, No. 1263, OECD Publishing, Paris, http://dx.doi.org/10.1787/5jrtpbnt7zf4-en.

Bassanini, A. and E. Caroli (2015), "Is Work Bad for Health? The Role of Constraint vs. Choice", *Annals of Economics and Statistics*, No. 119-120, pp. 13-37.

Bongaarts, J. (2001), "Household Size and Composition in the Developing World in the 1990s", *Population Studies*, Vol. 55, No. 3, pp. 263-279.

Campbell, J.C and N. Ikegami (2000), "Long-term Care Insurance Comes to Japan", *Health Affairs*, Vol. 19, pp. 26-39, http://content.healthaffairs.org/content/19/3/26.long.

Cingano, F. (2014), "Trends in Income Inequality and its Impact on Economic Growth", *OECD Social, Employment and Migration Working Papers*, No. 163, OECD Publishing, Paris, http://dx.doi.org/10.1787/5jxrjncwxv6j-en.

Compact 2025 (2016), "Bangladesh, Ending Hunger and Undernutrition Challenges and Opportunities, draft Scoping report for discussion, May, http://www.compact2025.org/files/2016/04/Bangladesh-Draft-Scoping-Report_FIN.pdf.

Government of Bangladesh (2017), "Second National Plan of Action for Nutrition 2016-2015", Dhaka.

Hussmanns, R. (2004), *Measuring the Informal Economy: From Employment in the Informal Sector to Informal Employment*, International Labour Office, Geneva.

ILO (2017), *The Main Drivers of Informality*, International Labour Office, Geneva, forthcoming.

ILO (2016a), *Word Employment and Social Outlook: Trends 2016*, International Labour Office, Geneva.

ILO (2016b), *Women at Work: Trends 2016*, International Labour Office, Geneva.

ILO (2015a), *World Employment and Social Outlook: The Changing Nature of Jobs*, International Labour Office, Geneva.

ILO (2013), *Women and Men in the Informal Economy: A Statistical Picture*, International Labour Organization Second edition (Geneva).

Jain-Chandra, S. et al. (2016), "Sharing the Growth Dividend: Analysis of Inequality in Asia", *IMF Working Paper WP/16/48*, International Monetary Fund, March.

Kim, H. (2016), "Korea Country Note", in A. Koslowski, S. Blum and P. Moss (eds.), *International Review of Leave Policies and Research 2016*, available at: http://www.oecd.org/els/family/publications.htm.

MHLW (2016), "Summary of Long-term Care Insurance and Future Challenges", Ministry of Health, Labour and Welfare, Tokyo, Japan, http://www.mhlw.go.jp/file/06-Seisakujouhou-12300000-Roukenkyoku/201602kaigohokenntoha_2.pdf.

MHLW (2012), "Future Projection of Costs Required for Social Security, 2012 March", Ministry of Health, Labour and Welfare, Tokyo, Japan, http://www.mhlw.go.jp/english/social_security/dl/social_security02.pdf.

Ministry of Gender Equality and Family Affairs (2016), "The Number of Children Using a Subsidised Personal Care Service in Korea" (in Korean), https://www.idolbom.go.kr/intro/index2.go.

Miranti, R. et al. (2013), "Trends in Poverty and Inequality in Decentralising Indonesia", *OECD Social, Employment and Migration Working Papers*, No. 148, OECD Publishing, Paris, http://dx.doi.org/10.1787/5k43bvt2dwjk-enOECD.

MOEL (2017), "Press Release on Fathers' Leave Taking, Rapidly Increasing", 24 January 2017, Ministry of Employment and Labour, Sejong-si, Korea.

MOEL (2016a), "Employment Insurance White Paper 2015", Ministry of Employment and Labour, Sejong-si, Korea.

MOEL (2016b), "Press Release on 2015 Take-up Rate of Child-related Leave", 4 February 2016, Ministry of Employment and Labour, Sejong-si, Korea.

MOEL (2010), "Employment Insurance White Paper 2009", Ministry of Employment and Labour, Seoul, Korea.

MOHW (2015), *Statistical Yearbook 2015*, Ministry of Health and Welfare, Sejong-si, Korea.

NIPSSR (2016), "Financial Statistics of Social Security in Japan", National Institute of Population and Social Security Research, Tokyo, http://www.ipss.go.jp/ss-cost/j/fsss-h26/fsss_h26.asp.

NIPSSR (2014), "Welfare for the Elderly, Social Security in Japan 2014", Chapter 5, National Institute of Population and Social Security Research, Tokyo, http://www.ipss.go.jp/s-info/e/ssj2014/index.asp.

OECD (2016a), "Backgrounder on Father's Leave and its Use", OECD Directorate for Employment, Labour and Social Affairs, Families and Children, OECD, Paris, www.oecd.org/els/family/Backgrounder-fathers-use-of-leave.pdf.

OECD (2016b), *Dare to Share, Germany's Experience Promoting Equal Partnership in Families*, OECD Publishing, Paris, http://dx.doi.org/10.1787/9789264259157-en.

OECD (2016c), "The OECD Gender Data Portal: Time Spent in Unpaid, Paid and Total Work, by Sex", OECD, Paris, www.oecd.org/gender/data/employment/.

OECD (2016d), *Employment Outlook 2016*, OECD Publishing, Paris, http://dx.doi.org/10.1787/empl_outlook-2016-en.

OECD (2015a), *OECD Economic Surveys: China 2015*, OECD Publishing, Paris, http://dx.doi.org/10.1787/eco_surveys-chn-2015-en.

OECD (2015b*), In It Together, Why Less Inequality Benefits All*, OECD Publishing, Paris, http://dx.doi.org/10.1787/9789264235120-en.

OECD (2015c), *Employment Outlook 2015*, OECD Publishing, Paris, http://dx.doi.org/10.1787/empl_outlook-2015-en.

OECD (2014a), "Social Spending Is Falling in Some Countries, But in Many Others It Remains at Historically High Levels", OECD Social Expenditure Database (SOCX) update, OECD, Paris, November, www.oecd.org/els/soc/OECD2014-Social-Expenditure-Update-Nov2014-8pages.pdf.

OECD (2014b), "Rising Inequality: Youth and Poor Fall Further Behind", Insights from the OECD Income Distribution Database, OECD, Paris, June, https://www.oecd.org/social/soc/inequality-publications.htm.

OECD (2014c), *Society at a Glance Asia/Pacific*, OECD Publishing, Paris, http://dx.doi.org/10.1787/9789264220553-en.

OECD (2014d), *OECD Economic Surveys: India 2014*, OECD Publishing, Paris, http://dx.doi.org/10.1787/eco_surveys-ind-2014-en.

OECD (2014e), *OECD Employment Outlook 2014*, OECD Publishing, Paris, http://dx.doi.org/10.1787/empl_outlook-2014-6-en.

OECD (2012), *Closing the Gender Gap: Act Now*, OECD Publishing, Paris, http://dx.doi.org/10.1787/9789264179370-en.

OECD (2011a), *Help Wanted, Providing and Paying for Long-term Care?*, Chapter 7: Public Long-term Care Financing Arrangements in OECD countries, OECD Publishing, Paris, http://www.oecd.org/els/health-systems/47884942.pdf.

OECD (2011b), *Society at a Glance Asia Pacific 2011*, OECD Publishing, Paris, http://dx.doi.org/10.1787/9789264106154-en.

OECD (2011c), *Doing Better for Families*, OECD Publishing, Paris, http://dx.doi.org/10.1787/9789264098732-en.

OECD Development Centre (2014a), *Social Institutions and Gender Index*, http://www.genderindex.org/.

OECD Development Centre (2014b), *Social Cohesion Policy Review of Viet Nam, Development Centre Studies*, OECD Publishing, Paris, http://dx.doi.org/10.1787/9789264196155-en.

OECD, ILO, IMF and World Bank (2014), "Achieving Stronger Growth by Promoting a More Gender-balanced Economy", August 15, http://www.oecd.org/g20/topics/employment-and-social-policy/ILO-IMF-OECD-WBG-Achieving-stronger-growth-by-promoting-a-more-gender-balanced-economy-G20.pdf.

Shi, L. and Z. Peng (2015), "Changes in Income Inequality in China in the Past Three Decades", Beijing Normal University, presentation at the 22nd International Research Conference of the Foundation for International Studies on Social Security (FISS), 7-9 June, Hong Kong (China).

Shi, L. and T. Sicula (2014), "The Distribution of Household Income in China: Inequality, Poverty and Policies", *The China Quarterly*, No. 217, March, pp. 1-41.

Shin, Y-j., J-e Yoo, H-y Kim and J-y Yoon (2013), "Comparative Study of Family Policy in East Asia – Korea, China, Japan and Singapore", OECD Korea Policy Centre, Koran Institute for Health and Social Affairs, Seoul.

Sorsa, P. et al. (2015), "Determinants of the Low Female Labour Force Participation in India", *OECD Economics Department Working Papers*, No. 1207, OECD Publishing, Paris, http://dx.doi.org/10.1787/5js30tvj21hh-en.

Stiglitz, J., A. Sen and J.P. Fitoussi (2009), "Report by the Commission on the Measurement of Economic Performance and Social Progress", http://www.stiglitz-sen-fitoussi.fr/documents/rapport_anglais.pdf.

Suh, M. and H. Lee (2014), "Financial Investment in Early Childhood Education and Care and its Impact in Korea: 2004-2014", Korea Institute of Child Care and Education, Seoul.

UNICEF (2016), "Child Mortality Estimates – Bangladesh", http://www.childmortality.org/, accessed 22 November 2016.

United Nations (2016), "United Nations Sustainable Development Knowledge Platform", https://sustainabledevelopment.un.org/topics/sustainabledevelopmentgoals (accessed 22 November 2016).

United Nations (2015), *World Population Prospects: The 2015 Revision*, Department of Economic and Social Affairs, Population Division New York, data accessed via http://esa.un.org/unpd/wpp/website.

VSS (2015), "Vietnam Social Security, 12/2015: VND 187 000 Billion Collected in 11 Months from Social Insurance and Health Insurance Contributions", http://www.baohiemxahoi.gov.vn/?u=nws&su=d&cid=384&id=13880, accessed on 8/1/2016.

Whiteford, P. and W. Adema (2007), "What Works Best in Reducing Child Poverty: A Benefit or Work Strategy?", *OECD Social, Employment and Migration Working Papers*, No. 51, OECD Publishing, Paris, http://dx.doi.org/10.1787/233310267230.

WHO (2014), "WHA Global Nutrition Targets 2025 – Stunting Policy Brief", http://www.who.int/nutrition/topics/globaltargets_stunting_policybrief.pdf, World Health Organisation, Geneva.

Zhuang, J. and L. Shi (2016), "Understanding the Recent Trend of Income Inequality in China", *SOAS Department of Economics Working Paper Series*, No. 196, the School of Oriental and African Studies, London.

Database references

OECD Income Distribution Database, http://www.oecd.org/social/income-distribution-database.htm.

OECD Education Database, http://www.oecd.org/education/database.htm

OECD Social Expenditure Database, www.oecd.org/social/expenditure.htm

OECD Family Database, http://www.oecd.org/social/family/database.htm

OECD Social Expenditure Database, http://www.oecd.org/social/expenditure.htm

Annex 1.A1
Background data to Chapter 1

Figure 1.A1.1. GDP growth in Asia and the OECD since 2000

Annual GDP growth rate (%)

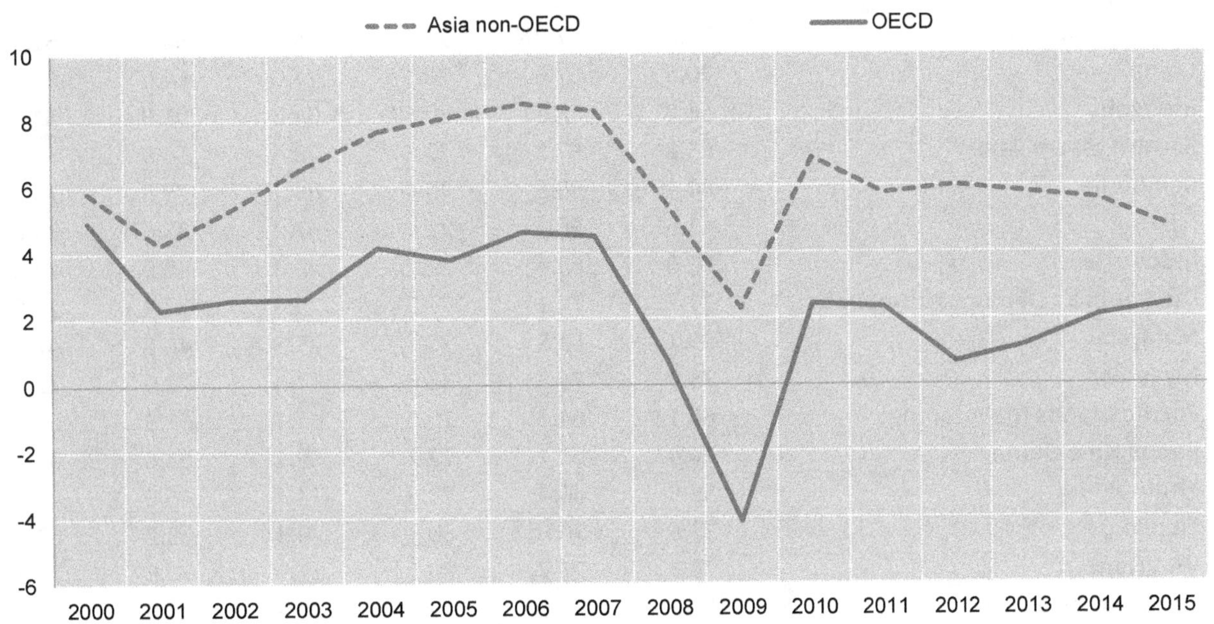

Source: World Bank, World Development Indicators, http://databank.worldbank.org/data/reports.aspx?source=world-development-indicators, as in October 2016. OECD (2015), *OECD Economic Outlook 97 Database*.

StatLink ⛬ http://dx.doi.org/10.1787/888933457405

Table 1.A1.1. Employment to population ratios, by gender 2005 and 2015

	Total		Male		Female	
	2005	2015	2005	2015	2005	2015
Developed Asia						
Australia	61.3	60.7	68.7	66.5	54.1	54.9
Hong Kong, China	57.5	58.3	66.6	66.0	49.4	51.7
Japan	57.8	57.3	70.0	67.7	46.4	47.6
Korea	58.7	58.6	69.7	69.1	47.9	48.3
New Zealand	64.7	63.6	72.2	69.3	57.8	58.3
Singapore	62.3	65.0	73.7	74.1	51.1	56.2
Developing Asia						
Eastern Asia	70.5	67.7	76.2	74.0	64.6	61.1
China	70.5	67.6	76.1	74.0	64.5	61.0
Mongolia	56.2	58.1	60.6	64.0	51.9	52.4
South-Eastern Asia	65.8	67.2	77.6	78.5	54.3	56.2
Cambodia	80.1	80.5	85.4	86.2	75.3	75.2
Fiji	53.6	50.2	71.0	67.0	35.6	33.0
Indonesia	60.0	63.4	77.2	79.3	42.9	47.5
Lao People's Democratic Republic	77.7	76.1	77.5	75.6	77.9	76.6
Malaysia	59.1	61.5	75.2	75.5	42.5	47.7
Myanmar	73.8	74.3	76.8	77.6	71.0	71.3
Pacific Islands (developing)	66.1	64.2	70.6	67.7	61.5	60.7
Papua New Guinea	70.4	68.1	72.2	69.1	68.6	67.1
Philippines	59.9	60.4	73.9	73.4	46.0	47.3
Thailand	72.6	70.6	80.3	79.3	65.2	62.3
Viet Nam	75.3	76.7	80.1	81.5	70.8	72.2
Southern Asia	57.7	52.8	79.7	76.8	34.6	27.6
Bangladesh	63.6	59.4	81.6	77.6	44.9	41.0
India	57.9	51.9	79.6	76.4	34.9	25.8
Nepal	82.2	80.5	86.3	83.8	78.4	77.5
Pakistan	48.9	51.0	79.0	78.7	16.9	22.0
Sri Lanka	50.6	49.3	71.9	73.1	30.3	27.9
Central and Western Asia	56.9	59.6	65.5	69.1	48.9	50.6
Armenia	47.7	53.0	57.3	62.9	39.0	44.9
Azerbaijan	58.7	61.9	62.2	65.6	55.4	58.4

Note: Sub regional estimates are based on the broader set of countries that form part of the sub region.

Source: ILO, Trends Econometric Models, October 2015; ILO Research Department.

StatLink ᴍᴙᴸ *http://dx.doi.org/10.1787/888933457559*

Chapter 2

Social protection expenditure and coverage across Asia

This chapter starts with setting out the scope of social expenditure and then summarises the prevalence of statutory social protection provisions across countries. The third section discusses issues around the extension the coverage of social protection benefits among elderly citizens considering pensions, non-contributory benefits as well as the Singaporean provident fund. Section 2.4 looks at the ADB's Social Protection Indicator to glean some insight in the extent to which richer and poorer countries devote resources to social expenditure and whether or not they are able to reach potential beneficiaries. This discussion illustrates the importance of different components of social spending (e.g., social insurance, social assistance, and active labour market programmes); and, the poverty and gender dimensions of distributional impacts of social spending.

This chapter also provides policy examples from countries to illustrate good practice, including on: employment retention subsidies in Korea; the Singaporean Central Provident Fund; the Zakat system in Malaysia; Indonesia's Unified Database and its plans to implement universal health insurance; and, Mongolia's Child Money Programme.

2.1   Introduction and main findings

Public social spending in Asia – not including OECD countries – is increasing and over the past ten years it has grown to almost 7% of GDP. Still, that is only a third of the OECD average at 21% of GDP. Relatively low prosperity levels in the past, the prevalence of informal employment and small shares of senior populations have so far curbed the growth of social expenditure in most Asian countries. Furthermore, in many Asian countries there is a strong sense of family commitment which often involves the provision of (care) support for elderly relatives (in-law), although this may have diminished over the years in more affluent countries such as Japan.

Social expenditure concerns the provision of supports household and individuals in need, and in terms of spending health issues and/or support in old age are main drivers of social spending, both in Asia as well as OECD countries. Other contingencies, such as unemployment benefits, labour market programmes, family allowances, maternity supports, social assistance benefits are much less widespread in Asia than in OECD countries.

This chapter starts with setting out the scope of social expenditure and then summarises the prevalence of statutory social protection provisions across countries. The third section discusses issues around the extension the coverage of social protection benefits among elderly citizens considering pensions, non-contributory benefits as well as the Singaporean provident fund. Section 2.4 looks at the ADB's Social Protection Indicator to glean some insight in the extent to which richer and poorer countries devote resources to social expenditure and whether or not they are able to reach potential beneficiaries. This discussion illustrates the importance of different components of social spending (e.g., social insurance, social assistance, and active labour market programmes); and, the poverty and gender dimensions of distributional impacts of social spending.

This chapter also provides policy examples from countries to illustrate good practice, including on: employment retention subsidies in Korea; the Singaporean Central Provident Fund; the Zakat system in Malaysia; Indonesia's Unified Database and its plans to implement universal health insurance; and, Mongolia's Child Money Programme.

Main findings

- Public social expenditure in Asia is on average 7% of GDP, but that is well below the OECD average at 21%. In Asia and the OECD outlays on social insurance (mainly pension and health insurance) benefits constitute the main part of public social expenditure in most countries. These contributory benefits are generally tied to formal employment, and as such are likely to benefit non-poor household rather than poor ones and men rather than women. Social assistance benefits may be available to the poorest households, especially if these are well targeted. However, the intensity of social assistance support may not be enough to lift households out of poverty, and many vulnerable low-income families receive very few, if any, benefits from either social insurance or social assistance.

- Some countries have tried to extend coverage of social insurance programmes, and such efforts were arguably most successful in China. However, many countries find it very difficult to effectively increase coverage of social insurance schemes for practical reasons. The administrative capacity is often lacking to register participants in insurance schemes and/or collect contributions from employers and employees.

- There is a growing role for non-contributory type old age allowances and some Asian countries have established non-contributory pension schemes with widespread coverage, as the main and sometimes only system of income provision in retirement.

- Countries such as Indonesia, Pakistan and the Philippines have substantial Conditional Cash Transfer programmes whilst India has a national employment guarantee programme. Nevertheless, in many Asian countries the share of non-contributory social assistance type expenditures to GDP is less than 0.5% of GDP. Non-contributory social assistance-type programmes appear underdeveloped in Asia, which may be somewhat surprising since the international development community and many national governments have prioritised poverty reduction since the 1990s. Political will has not been strong enough to translate into effective anti-poverty measures that tie in with the economic growth that trickles down to reduce (extreme) poverty. Public spending on such programmes is limited, and the associated low payment rates raise concerns about the adequacy of such benefits.

- The expenditure for labour market programmes, including food for work programmes, in Asia is very small e.g., less than 0.1% as share to GDP. Passive labour market programmes such as unemployment benefits or severance payments for formal workers might be important in some high income countries such as Japan, Korea and Singapore; they are virtually non-existent in most middle-income countries.

- Extending social assistance and social insurance schemes is needed to reduce poverty and provide for the increasing medical and income needs of ageing populations increase. Investment in children, whether or not by means of conditional cash transfers, and associated health and early and primary education services is key. Greater investment in active labour market programmes would provide informal workers and the poor and vulnerable population with greater access to employment guarantee schemes or skill development and training.

2.2.   The scope of social protection

For the discussion of spending trends access to, coverage by, and the prevalence of social protection arrangements, it is important to frame some relevant concepts: The OECD defines social expenditures as:

"The provision by public and private institutions of benefits to, and financial contributions targeted at, households and individuals in order to provide support during circumstances which adversely affect their welfare, provided that the provision of the benefits and financial contributions constitutes neither a direct payment for a particular good or service nor an individual contract or transfer."

Since only benefits provided by institutions are included in the social expenditure definition, transfers between households – albeit of a social nature, are not in the social domain. This is important as in Asia support between family members (often living together) is an important part of the social fabric.

Broadly speaking there are two main criteria which have to be simultaneously satisfied for a programme to be classified as social: the programme has to redistribute resources across people and has to serve a social purpose (see Adema et al., 2011, for more detail). The inter-personal redistribution of resources is often brought about by compulsory participation or by public financing of social benefits. For example, a health insurance programme that requires all covered workers to make contributions to the benefit plan regardless of their health status.

In this case redistribution works through the risk profile – the risk of falling ill is being shared – but the amount of redistribution can also be altered by programme characteristics as benefit caps, or increased contribution rates for workers in higher earnings groups, etc. The redistributive nature of a social programme is most evident when support is provided for free or at sharply reduced prices, e.g. subsidised food programmes or free medical aid, but also the provision of income support under minimum living standard schemes in China, Japan or Korea. Increasingly, the provision of social assistance types of support is linked to certain conditions, as participation in health programmes or education (see Barrientos, 2013 for a full discussion).

Also, the benefits provided have to be intended to address one or more social purposes. There are different categorisations of social support (OECD, 2016a; ADB, 2016; Eurostat, 2012; and, ILO, 2005), but they generally include:[1]

- support for the elderly and pensions for old age and/or survivors,

- incapacity related benefits, including invalidity benefits, benefits accruing from occupational injury and accident legislation, and employee sickness payments,

- family benefits– child allowances, childcare support, and income support during maternity leave,

- housing allowances and rent subsidies,

- unemployment compensation and active labour market policies – employment services, training, employment incentives, integration of the disabled, direct job creation, and start-up incentives,

- health supports as in- and out-patient care, medical goods, and health prevention.

These social benefits can be provided in "cash" (e.g., old age pension payments, income support during maternity leave and social assistance payments) and "in-kind" (e.g., services as medical interventions, childcare supports or care supports for the elderly and disabled). Social support can also be delivered through the tax system (for example, favourable tax treatment of families with children or contributions to private pension plans). In Asia, this manner of providing social support is most prevalent in higher income countries such as Japan and Korea.

Statutory provisions

The arrangements for the provision of social benefits are often laid down in national legislation, which Table 2.1 provides an overview of the existence of arrangements by a range of benefits. Employment injury compensation exists in all countries in Asia. Old age, survivors and disability protection also exists in all Asian countries but while legal provisions are in place Cambodia and Myanmar have yet to introduce national pension schemes for formal workers in the private sectors.

Table 2.1. Do statutory social protection provisions exist?

Number and type of areas covered by at least one social protection programme

Country	Number of policy areas covered by at least one programme		Existence of a statutory programme							
	Number of policy areas covered by at least one programme	Number of social security policy areas covered by a statutory programme | Strict definition	Sickness (cash)	Maternity (cash)	Old age	Employment injury	Invalidity	Survivors	Family allowances	Unemployment
Armenia	8	Comprehensive scope of legal coverage | 8	●	●	●	●	●	●	●	●
Australia	8	Comprehensive scope of legal coverage | 8	●	●	●	●	●	●	●	●
Azerbaijan	8	Comprehensive scope of legal coverage | 8	●	●	●	●	●	●	●	●
Bangladesh	4	Very limited scope of legal coverage | 1 to 4	●	●	●	●	None	None	None	▲
Cambodia	1	Very limited scope of legal coverage | 1 to 4	None	▲	⌂	●	⌂	⌂	None	▲
China	8	Comprehensive scope of legal coverage | 8	●	●	●	●	●	●	●	●
Fiji	5	Limited scope of legal coverage | 5 to 6	None	▲	●	●	●	●	●	None
Hong Kong, China	8	Comprehensive scope of legal coverage | 8	●	●	●	●	●	●	●	●
India	7	Semi-comprehensive scope | 7	●	●	●	●	●	●	None	●
Indonesia	4	Very limited scope of legal coverage | 1 to 4	△	▲	●	●	●	●	None	▲
Japan	8	Comprehensive scope of legal coverage | 8	●	●	●	●	●	●	●	●
Korea[1]	5	Limited scope of legal coverage | 5 to 6	●	▲	●	●	●	●	None	●
Lao PDR	6	Limited scope of legal coverage | 5 to 6	●	●	●	●	●	●	None	⌂
Malaysia	4	Very limited scope of legal coverage | 1 to 4	△	▲	●	●	●	●	None	▲
Mongolia	8	Comprehensive scope of legal coverage | 8	●	●	●	●	●	●	●	●
Myanmar[2]	3	Very limited scope of legal coverage | 1 to 4	●	●	⌂	●	⌂	⌂	⌂	⌂
Nepal	4	Very limited scope of legal coverage | 1 to 4	▲	▲	●	●	●	●	None	▲
New Zealand	8	Comprehensive scope of legal coverage | 8	●	●	●	●	●	●	●	●
Pakistan	6	Limited scope of legal coverage | 5 to 6	●	●	●	●	●	●	None	▲
Papua New Guinea	4	Very limited scope of legal coverage | 1 to 4	▲	None	●	●	●	●	None	None
Philippines	6	Limited scope of legal coverage | 5 to 6	●	●	●	●	●	●	None	▲
Singapore	5	Semi-comprehensive scope | 7	▲	▲	●	●	●	●	●	None
Sri Lanka	5	Limited scope of legal coverage | 5 to 6	△	▲	●	●	●	●	●	▲
Thailand	8	Comprehensive scope of legal coverage | 8	●	●	●	●	●	●	●	●
Viet Nam	7	Semi-comprehensive scope | 7	●	●	●	●	●	●	None	●

Symbols

●	At least one programme anchored in national legislation
⌂	Programme has yet to be implemented.
▲	Limited provisions via employer's liability under national labour code (includes company sick leave and severance pay
△	Only benefit in kind (e.g. medical benefit).

"..." Not available.

The scope of social security legal coverage as based on number of social security policy areas covered by a statutory programme: "very limited" (1 to 4 policy areas); "limited" (5 to 6 policy areas); "semi-comprehensive" (7 policy areas); and "comprehensive" (8 policy areas).

1. Korea has a child allowance for home-care that was introduced for households with children under 6 who do not use childcare facilities or kindergartens (Chapter 1, Box 1.2).

2. Myanmar enacted its social security law in 2012, but the all relevant provisions have not yet been implemented.

Source: US SSA (2015), "Social Security Programs throughout the World: Asia and the Pacific 2014"; ILO (2015), "NORMLEX: Information System on International Labour Standards", available online at http://www.ilo.org/dyn/normlex/en/; and, ILO (2015), *The State of Social Protection in ASEAN at the Dawn of Integration*.

Most countries, except Papua New Guinea, have legislation that provides for income support in case of absence from work because of maternity or sickness. However, in eight countries such payments are responsibility of the employers subject to regulations in national labour codes rather than social protection legislation. Family cash allowances regarding dependent children (up to age 15+) do not exist in Bangladesh, Cambodia, India, Indonesia, Korea, Lao PDR, Malaysia, Myanmar, Nepal, Papua New Guinea, Pakistan, the Philippines and Viet Nam. Similarly, many Asian countries do not have legislation that provides for regular payment of unemployment benefits, but severance payment provisions exist in Bangladesh, Cambodia, Indonesia Korea, Malaysia, Nepal, Pakistan, the Philippines and Sri Lanka. Overall, it seems that in South Asia and the Pacific social protection systems are still at a relatively early stage of development in contrast to Armenia, Azerbaijan, China, Mongolia, Thailand and the OECD countries in the region (Table 2.1).

However, the fact that legal provisions are in place does not mean that all groups of workers are covered by these provisions. For example, the legal coverage rates of employment injury schemes range from less than 10% of the labour force in Nepal, Lao PDR or India to more than 85% in Japan, Korea and Hong Kong (China) (ILO, 2014 and 2015a). The main reason for this is that the self-employed and other groups of workers (e.g. short-term workers, or employees in small, medium enterprises) often make up the majority of workers and are not covered by the legal provisions (ILO, 2015c and 2016a). Box 2.1 provides information on the coverage of unemployment benefits under the Employment Insurance system in Korea.

Box 2.1. Employment Insurance in Korea

Korea's Employment Insurance System (EIS), launched in 1995, consists of unemployment benefit, job security programmes and job capability development programmes. Unemployment Benefit is to assist workers who have lost their jobs and help them find a new job. Apart from the traditional income support function, the EIS includes programmes to reduce likelihood of unemployment and increase employability of employees. The job security programme aims to create new jobs and to encourage employers to retain their employees rather than laying them off. The job capability development programme provides various opportunities in training and education to improve employees' productivity and earnings as well as corporate competitiveness.

The "job-seekers allowance" is the main part of unemployment benefit. To be eligible for this benefit, employees must have been insured for 180 days during the 18 months prior to unemployment. The payment rate of the "job-seekers allowance is 50% of the average wage during the three months before the person became unemployed with a minimum payment of 90% of the legal minimum daily wage or USD 39 per day in 2016. The duration of benefit receipt is determined by both the age of and the insurance period of the recipient. The minimum duration is 90 days for those under the age of 30 and an insured period of less than a year; the maximum duration is 240 days for those age 50 and above with an insured period of ten years or more.

The EIS played an important role in cushioning the impact of economic crises in Korea. The subsidy for employment retention is a good example. This subsidy is granted to employers who keep on employees by relocating their positions or providing them with training opportunities etc., rather than laying them off. During the two economic crises – 1998 Asian crisis and, especially the Great Recession (2008/09) –, public spending on the subsidy increased markedly (Figure 2.1), which contributed to preventing widespread unemployment. In 2009, the amount of spending on the employment retention subsidy increased tenfold compared to the previous year (MOEL, 2009 and 2015).

Korea's Employment Insurance started with firms with 30 employees and more in 1995, and its legal coverage has extended to workplaces with 1 or more worker in 1998, and then finally to daily workers in 2004. With this expansion of the scope of beneficiaries, the number of establishments covered increased from 400 000 (in 1998) to 2 million in 2014, while the number of insured persons increased from 5.2 million to 11.9 million in 2014 (MOEL, 2009 and 2015).

Box 2.1. Employment Insurance in Korea *(cont.)*

However, there are still many workers who are not covered by the EIS. The EIS does not apply to businesses in the agriculture, forestry, fishery, and hunting sectors with four or less employees and small construction enterprises. Governmental officials, teachers, and those working less than 60 hours per month (If part-time workers working less than 60 hours per month continue to work three months and more, they can apply for coverage by EIS) and domestic workers are also excluded. Besides these business and workers who are exempted by regulation, there are employers and workers – often in small firms – who do not pay EI contributions. In 2014, among all the legally eligible workers for the EIS, 26% (around 4 million) were not insured (Yoo and Choi, 2014). There is a substantial coverage gap between regular workers (with a permanent, open-ended contract) and non-regular workers with employment contracts of a limited duration (fixed-term, part-time and "dispatch workers" who have an employment contract with a temporary work agency). In 2015, almost all regular workers were covered by the EIS, only 63% of the non-regular workers were covered (OECD, 2016b). It is essential to increase compliance with contributory rules and weaken incentives to hire non-regular workers. The Durunuri programme was introduced to reduce the burden of insurance premiums of the EIS for small firms in 2013. This subsidises 50% of National Pension and Employment Insurance premiums for both employers and employees, when the employees' wage (in 2015) is less than KRW 1 400 000 (USD 1 253 per month).

Figure 2.1. Spending on the subsidy for employment retention in Korea increased during the Great Recession

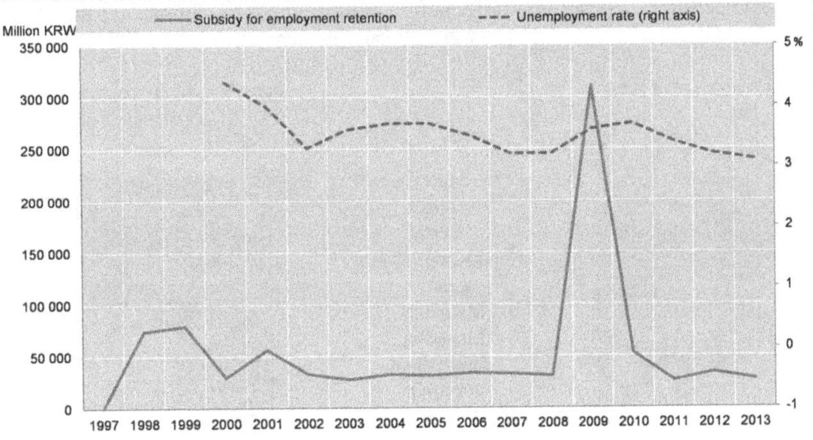

Source: MOEL (2009 and 2015).

StatLink ⓘ *http://dx.doi.org/10.1787/888933457416*

Extending coverage to more people: the case of pensions and income support for the elderly

In view of population ageing in Asia, the lack of long term pension coverage – the number of people in the labour force and/or the working age population who contribute to a mandatory pensions system – is a key policy challenge. Many Asian countries have a long-term pension coverage problem in that only 40% of the labour force participants contribute to a pension system and this is often around 20% or less of the working-age population: in Indonesia, India, Papua New Guinea, Bangladesh, Lao PDR, Cambodia, Nepal and Pakistan less than 10% of working age population is covered by a pension programme (Figure 2.2). In all, not many future senior citizens will have built up an entitlement to a pension, and this risk is highest in low-income countries. This contributes to a very high risk of old-age poverty in these countries and Bangladesh, India, Lao PDR and Pakistan all have at least 60% of their populations trying to get by on less than USD 2 per day (Figure 2.2).

Since 1990, many countries in Asia have introduced new measures to provide cash payments for people in retirement and/or extend coverage of pension schemes among the population. But among Asian countries, the extension of pension coverage has been most pronounced in China. Next to pension provision for civil servants and other public service unit workers, 1997 pension reform in China established a national multi-pillar pension system with the aim to cover all employees working in urban areas (Salditt et al., 2008). Over the years this system has culminated into the present basic urban worker pension system (BUWPS), and the coverage rate (the number of participants relative to the number of workers), increased from 60% in 2005 to 88% in 2015 (Queisser et al., 2016). Furthermore, the 2009 introduction of the "new rural co-operative pension scheme", and the 2011 introduction of the "urban resident pension scheme" extended coverage to population groups hitherto not covered. Various measures were introduced to encourage coverage, including subsidised contributions, and making pension payments to elderly parents of working-age adults who started to make contributions to a rural pension scheme (ILO, 2014). These two schemes have now been merged into a basic national resident pensions system which in 2015 covered 505 million people.

Figure 2.2. Pension coverage highest among workers in high and middle income countries

Active contributors to old age pension scheme (periodic benefits) as percent of the labour force and the working age population (2015 or latest available year)

Panel A. Active contributors to a pension scheme in the labour force 15+ (%)

Panel B. Active contributors to a pension scheme in the working-age population 15–64 (%)

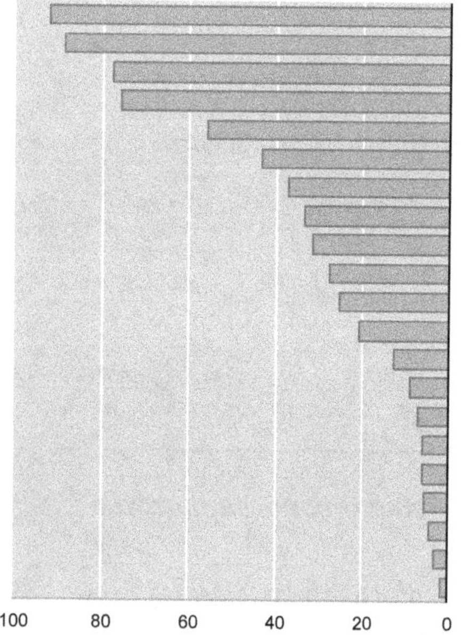
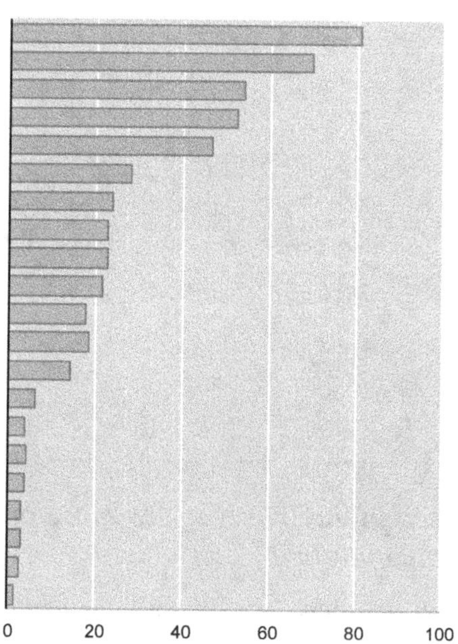

1. This would be zero if only periodic cash benefits were considered; lump sum payments from provident funds are included here.

Source: ILO Social Protection database and ILO (2015), *World Employment and Social Outlook*; for Japan: MHLW (2015), "Comprehensive Survey of Living Conditions".

StatLink 🔗 *http://dx.doi.org/10.1787/888933457428*

The pension replacement rate, i.e. the ratio of the pension benefit to previous earnings, provides some indication on the degree to which retirees will see their pre-retirement living standards preserved through the pension system (the underlying OECD methodology is laid out in OECD, 2015a). Figure 2.3 suggests that that if all assumptions are met – an uninterrupted career in formal employment for 35 years as from age 20, the gross replacement are across the OECD would be around 55% for those on average earnings, and gross replacement rates in Asian pension systems are generally below those in OECD countries. The replacement rates in China and Viet Nam, Pakistan and India compare favourably with those in OECD countries on average. However, it should be emphasised that these projections, assume that workers contributed for a full career to the pension system; while this may be the case for some groups of urban workers, this is unlikely to concern the majority of workers.

Furthermore, Figure 2.3 also gives an indication on the redistributive nature of many pension systems means that pension replacement rates are higher for low-income earners. Pensions systems in Indonesia, Hong Kong (China), Malaysia, Singapore, Sri Lanka, Thailand and Viet Nam do not appear to be redistributive as gross replacement rates are the same for low and average earners alike.

Figure 2.3. Most pensions systems have higher replacement rates for low-income earners

Gross replacement rates at average and low earnings, percentage

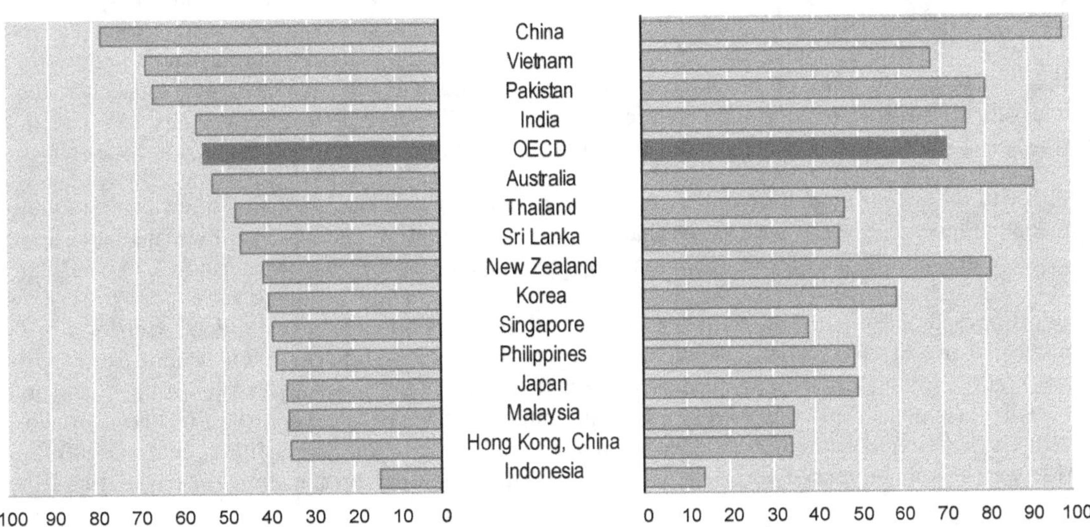

Note: The gross (before tax) replacement rate used here shows the pension benefit as a share of individual lifetime average earnings (re-valued in line with economy-wide earnings growth, in this case at individual lifetime average earnings and low earnings (50% of average earnings). Under the baseline assumptions, workers earn the same percentage of average earnings throughout their career (in this case, lifetime average re-valued earnings and individual final earnings are identical). It is assumed that workers have an uninterrupted work history, from age 20 until the pensionable age.

Source: OECD (2013), *Pensions at a Glance Asia/Pacific 2013*.

StatLink ᵐˢᵖ *http://dx.doi.org/10.1787/888933457432*

Other challenges that pension systems face include the withdrawal of savings before retirement age and/or, taking pensions out as lump sum rather than regular payments (so that people can outlive their resources) and the non-indexation of pension payments (OECD, 2013). In addition, retirement ages are often well below 65, especially for women, which can affect the financial sustainability of systems as well as the adequacy of retirement benefits. Figure 2.2 suggests that pension coverage is strongly associated with level of economic development (also see Figure 2.A1.1 in Annex 2.A1). As economic growth in Asia is projected on a lower path than in the recent past, pension coverage is unlikely to rapidly increase unless governments can effectively introduce mandatory pension systems.

Box 2.2. Singapore Central Provident Fund (CPF)

The Singapore Central Provident Fund (CPF) – an asset-based mandatory contributory social protection scheme – is a key pillar of Singapore's social protection system. Singapore introduced the CPF with the aim to provide its people a safety net against soaring living and housing costs and help them to meet growing retirement and health care needs.

The monthly tax-exempted contributions, funded by employers and employees, are deposited into three accounts; the Ordinary Account, the Special Account and the Medisave Account. These savings can be withdrawn to meet approved housing, investment, health care, own or immediate family's education and retirement costs. At the age of 55, a Retirement account is automatically created and money is pooled from the Ordinary and Special account to meet the Minimum Sum required which serves to pay a monthly retirement benefit to the person as from pay-out eligibility age of 65 years old until the account is depleted, generally at 85 years old. Members receive a fixed interest rate of 2.5% on their Ordinary account and 4% interest on the other accounts.

CPF members can make pre-retirement withdrawals to pay for down-payments, stamp duties, mortgage payments and interest incurred for the housing purchases. CPF funds are often used for this purpose and the programme has been successful in encouraging home ownership. With respect to health care, beyond the coverage of the basic Medisave account, a low cost catastrophic medical insurance scheme, MediShield has been put in place to allow for risk-pooling against major illnesses. In view of increased life expectancy and late life medical costs, the latter was replaced by MediShield Life in 2015 to provide lifelong protection at an affordable premium, whereby low and middle-income earners are subsidised by the government and there exists additional premium support to ensure better coverage.

The adequacy of the CPF system in covering retirement and health care needs is being questioned, in view of the need for retirement support and health care needs that come with population ageing: Singaporeans have the third highest life expectancy at birth: 83.1 years in 2015, only the Swiss (83.4 years) and Japanese (83.7 years) can on average expect to live longer at birth (WHO, 2016). CPF savings can provide adequate retirement provisions for young Singaporeans comparable to outcomes in OECD countries if individuals made prudent decisions in their housing consumption and use of CPF savings. However, many Singaporeans withdraw their wealth from the CPF prior to retirement. Figure 2.4 illustrates the increasing trend in the ratio of the net withdrawals from to contributions to the CPF in recent years and in 2015 net withdrawals amounted to over half the contributions paid in. To increase the available funds in retirement, the government has put in place an optional CPF-LIFE scheme in 2009, mandatory as from 2013, which is an advanced life deferred annuity with flexibility on the monthly pay-out and the amount of bequest to beneficiaries.

Another issue relates to the limited coverage of non-residents including short-term workers and their families, foreign domestic workers and foreign students, which constitute a significant share of the population: almost 30% of the total population in 2014 and around 40% of the working population were "non-resident" (DOS, 2015). On the other hand, new initiatives are being undertaken to redistribute incomes to older, low wage earners and other vulnerable groups, to ensure greater inclusiveness of the economic growth (Sharma, 2014).

On the whole, in terms of social policy, the Singapore Government sees its role more as a regulatory body than a direct welfare service provider (Mendes, 2009). The notion of independence through reliance on work rather than dependence on welfare schemes is encouraged, which helps to explain the absence of minimum wage regulations and unemployment benefit programmes as exist in most advanced economies. The government has established provisions based on strict eligibility criteria to help individuals in need and increase employability through its workfare approach. To provide greater support to low-income earners, their CPF savings are supplemented by the government through the Workfare scheme and top-ups are made to the Medisave account of senior citizens.

Box 2.2. Singapore Central Provident Fund (CPF) *(cont.)*

Figure 2.4. Net withdrawals were over half of all contributions paid, in 2015

Trend in the Ratio of net amount withdrawn to the CPF contributions received

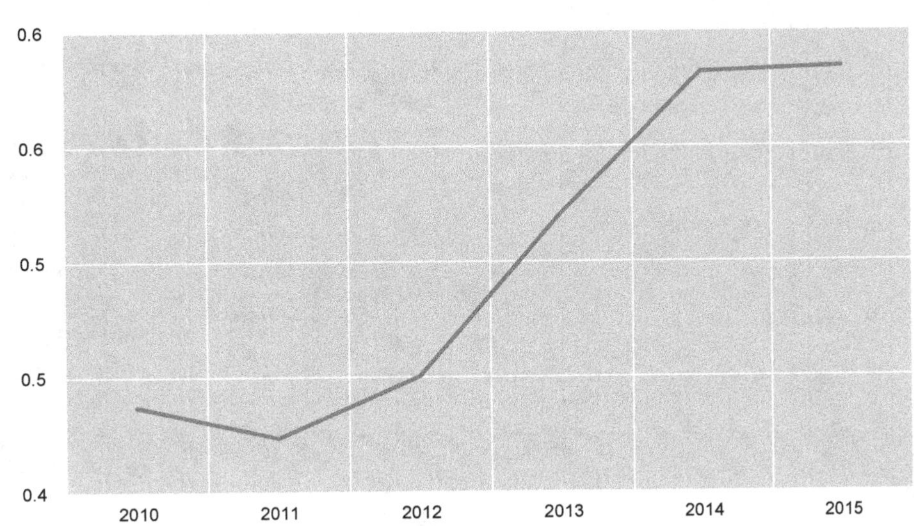

Source: Central Provident Fund Board, data retrieved from: https://data.gov.sg/dataset/total-net-cpf-contributions-received-total-net-amount-withdrawn-in-year?resource_id=23d7cbf8-bea7-410e-a939-5921014a31fc (10 October 2016).

StatLink *http://dx.doi.org/10.1787/888933457444*

Many people of working age in Asian countries are exposed to income insecurity in the future

Various countries have introduced cash support for old-age citizens on basis of non-contributory periodic payments (e.g. Bangladesh (1998), India (1995), Indonesia (2006), Nepal (1995) and Viet Nam (2004/05), see also ADB, 2012), either as a complementary payment from contributory pension schemes or as a separate programme. Means-tested or not, these non-contributory programmes often have a direct effect on the proportion of the elderly population who receive some sort of periodic income support in old age (Figure 2.5), perhaps not so much in Indonesia, where coverage of the 2006 Programme Jaminan Sosial Lanjut Usia (Elderly Social Security Programme) remains limited. Since 1995 the poor in India can receive support through the Indira Gandhi National Old Age Pension Scheme (IGNOAPS). In 2011, the eligibility age was reduced from 65 to 60, as payment rates for those aged 80 or older were raised. India has about 80 million persons aged 60 or older, of which 51 million with incomes below the poverty line (ISSA, 2013).

Figure 2.5. In most low and medium income countries in Asia most elderly do not receive a pension or a non-contributory cash payment

Old age pension recipients as a percent of the number of people above the statutory retirement age, around 2010/11

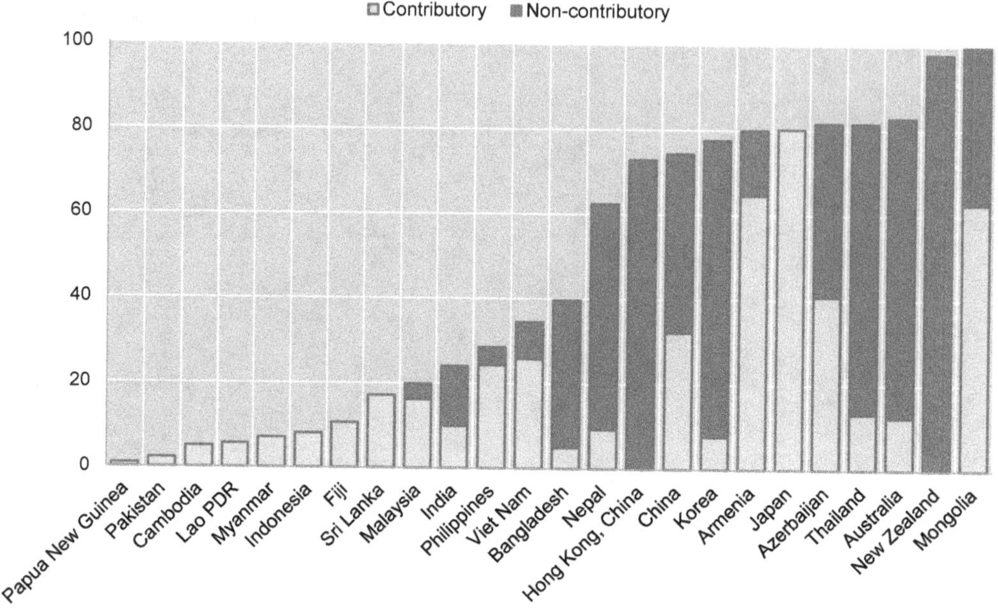

Source: HelpAge International: Help Age's social pensions database (http://www.pension-watch.net/about-social-pensions/about-social-pensions/social-pensions-database).

StatLink ᴍᴸᴾ *http://dx.doi.org/10.1787/888933457457*

In some other Asian countries, a significant proportion of senior citizens now receive a "non-contributory periodic old age payment" (Figure 2.5). Such payments cover about 33% of senior citizens in Bangladesh; and around 50% in Nepal (introduction in 1995). In Thailand, the Old Age Allowance introduced in 1993 reached close to 70% of the population aged 60 and over in 2011, and almost three/quarters of the elderly in Hong Kong (China) receive the Old Age Allowance. Similarly, the Basic Old-age Pension introduced in 2008 in Korea, reaches about 70% of the people aged 65 and over and provides KRW 200 000 (about USD 180) per month per beneficiary on average. Often these concern social assistance type payments that are phased out or withdrawn against other sources of income (e.g. earnings or pension payments) but not with basic pensions in China and the Philippines (OECD, 2013).

However, payment rates under these social assistance type income support schemes for the elderly are low and well below the replacement rates that can be achieved on basis of complete contributory records to public pension schemes (Figure 2.3 above). In eight of the 19 Asian countries with a non-contributory pension (for which data are available), beneficiaries receive less than USD PPP 1.25 (purchasing power parity) a day, and in 11 out of 19 countries, this is less than USD PPP 2 a day (ILO, 2015a). Nevertheless, these programmes can play a role in poverty reduction. For example, in Thailand, the old-age allowance (Bia Yung Cheep) contributed to a decline in the poverty rate of elderly single-person households (from 5.8% to 2.5%) and a fall in the poverty rate of all households from 9.6%t to 8.3% (ILO, 2015a).

2.3.   Social protection expenditure trends

Public social spending in the Asian region (on average around 7% of GDP) was less than a third of the OECD average (21.1%) in 2013 (Figure 2.6), but in Bangladesh, Indonesia, Cambodia, India, Pakistan, Lao PDR and Myanmar it amounted to less than 3% of GDP. In many Asian countries, social insurance systems (and income tax systems, see Box 2.3) have not developed comprehensively as coverage is limited to only a small portion of the (working-age) population. However, the relatively low level of public social spending implies that a large number of people who are vulnerable to social risks such as poverty, illness, disability and unemployment receive little or no support.

Then again, in most Asian countries public investment in social expenditure (not including education) has increased since the turn of the millennium, except in Azerbaijan, Sri Lanka and Lao PDR. Public social expenditure-to-GDP ratios increased by more than 3 percentage points in Armenia, China, Malaysia, Mongolia, Thailand and Singapore (Figure 2.6). The OECD average increased by almost 3 percentage points since 2000, but because of ongoing population ageing in combination with limited economic (GDP) growth, the public social spending to GDP ratio in Japan increased considerable (7 percentage points). Over the same period, public social spending to GDP almost doubled in Korea (an increase by about 5 percentage points).

Figure 2.6. Public social spending is increasing in Asia

Trends in public social protection spending as a percent of GDP, 2000 and 2013/14 or latest year

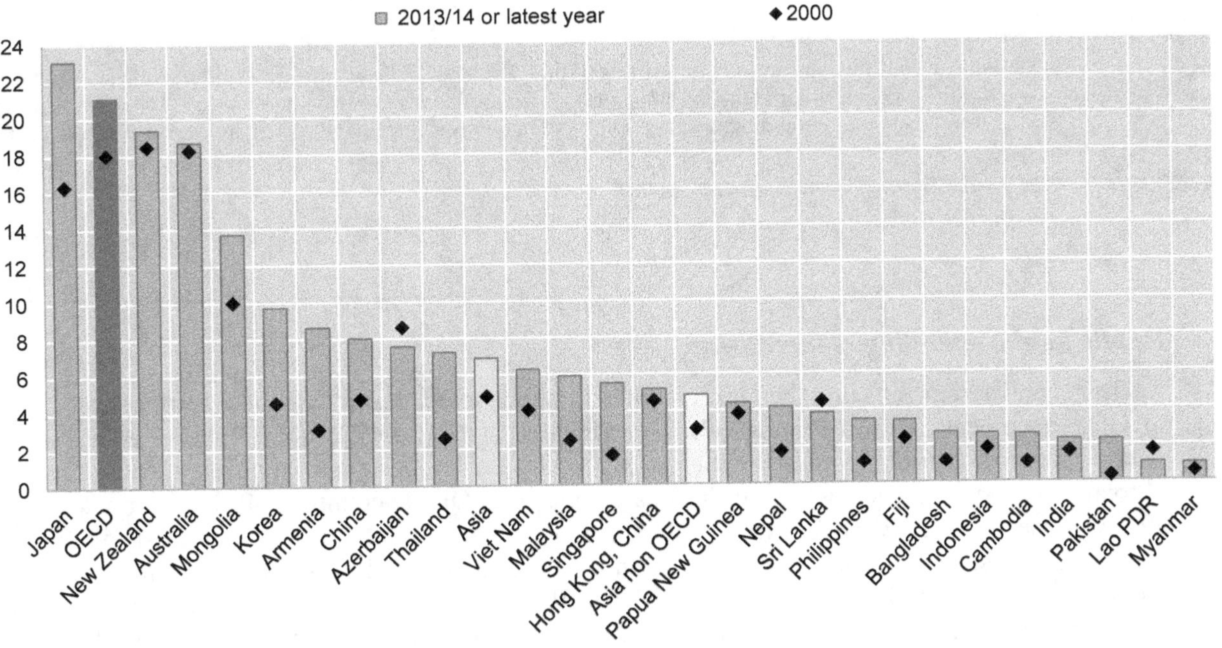

Source: ILO,   *The   World   Social   Protection   Report   2014-15*,   http://www.social-protection.org/gimi/gess/ShowTheme.action?th.themeId=3985, ADB staff estimates based on country reports Social Protection Indicator,   2015,   World   Health   Organisation   Database   (WHO),   *OECD   Social   Expenditure   Database* (http://www.oecd.org/social/expenditure.htm).

StatLink ᴍᴍᴘ *http://dx.doi.org/10.1787/888933457468*

Box 2.3. Tax-to-GDP ratios

The differences in social spending levels between Asian countries and OECD countries are mirrored in differences in Tax revenues (Table 2.2 and OECD, 2016c) Tax-to-GDP ratios in Indonesia, Malaysia, the Philippines and Singapore ranged from 12 to 17% of GDP in 2014; about half of Tax-to-GDP ratios in Australia, Japan and New Zealand. The OECD average lies around 34% since 2000, and in many European countries the tax intake is considerably higher. In 2014, the tax-to-GDP ratios were highest in France and Denmark at around 46% of GDP respectively (OECD, 2016d). In Denmark, direct taxation of benefit payments and indirect taxation of consumption was worth about 8% of GDP in 2013 (see OECD, 2016d and Adema et al., 2011 for the underlying methodology). Because of taxation of benefit income and associated consumption, social effort in European countries is often considerably lower than what gross (before tax) public social expenditure-to-GDP ratios as in Figure 2.6 suggest.

Table 2.2. Tax revenue in Asia countries is well below the OECD average

Tax revenue-to-GDP ratios, 1990-2014

	1990	1995	2000	2005	2008	2009	2010	2011	2012	2013	2014
Indonesia[1]	..	..	8.6	13.5	14.2	11.9	11.4	12.2	12.5	12.5	12.2
Malaysia[2]	19.1	19.9	14.6	16.1	15.7	16.1	14.4	15.8	16.6	16.3	15.9
Philippines	..	16.2	15.8	15.2	16.2	15.0	14.8	15.1	15.8	16.2	16.7
Singapore	..	..	15.5	12.1	13.9	13.1	13.0	13.3	13.9	13.6	13.9
OECD[3]	32.2	33.6	34.3	33.6	33.2	32.4	32.6	33.0	33.4	33.8	34.2
Japan	28.5	26.4	26.6	27.3	28.5	27.0	27.6	28.6	29.5	30.3	32.0
Korea	18.8	19.0	21.5	22.5	24.6	23.8	23.4	24.2	24.8	24.3	24.6
Australia	28.1	28.2	30.4	29.9	27.0	25.8	25.6	26.3	27.3	27.5	..
New Zealand	36.2	35.6	32.5	36.0	33.3	30.5	30.6	30.9	32.4	31.4	..

1. The figures for social security contributions are not available, but they are thought to be negligible as they relate only to the "Asuransi Kesehatan" – a health insurance programme for employees in for-profit state-owned enterprises. 2. The figures include local government taxes. 3. Represents the unweighted average for OECD countries. Japan and Korea are also part of the OECD group of 35 countries.

Source: OECD (2016), *Revenue Statistics in Asian Countries 2016*.

StatLink ᴍᴤᴘ *http://dx.doi.org/10.1787/888933457578*

Public health spending is increasing

In general across Asia and the OECD trends in public expenditure on health as a percent of GDP have been upward (Figure 2.7). Nevertheless, at 6% of GDP the OECD average public spending on health is twice as high as across Asia. Also, the share of public spending in total health spending is much lower in Asia compared to OECD countries: 48.1% vis-a-vis 72.7% respectively (OECD, 2014a). Public financial resources for health differ markedly across countries: they are highest in Japan and New Zealand at close to 8% of GDP and around 1% of GDP in Bangladesh, Lao PDR and Pakistan. Public expenditure on health is increasing in Japan with population ageing. In some other Asian countries, public health spending is increasing too, including in China and Viet Nam, where this is, in part, related to the extension of health insurance coverage. Public expenditure on health is also expected to increase in Indonesia with the rolling out of universal health coverage (Box 2.4).

Countries in the Asia/Pacific region are diverse, and their health issues and health systems are often very different. However, there are some common trends. As illustrated above, gains in life expectancy have been substantial. Furthermore, the infant mortality rate has fallen dramatically across the region since 1990, with many countries experiencing declines of greater than 50%. Nevertheless at an average of 23 deaths per 1 000 live births in 2012 infant mortality is still six times the OECD rate. Similarly, the average maternal mortality rate in Asia has been cut by 48% between 1990 and 2013, but is still 15 times higher than across the OECD (OECD, 2014a). Other issues in health include improving sanitation in rural areas, reducing the high smoking rate, especially for men, and a relatively limited supply of doctors and nurses in the region. There also seems to be growing interest in the development and assessment of quality of health care in the region (OECD, 2016e).

Figure 2.7. Public health spending is increasing but still twice as high in the OECD as across Asia

General government expenditure on health as % of GDP (2005, 2014)

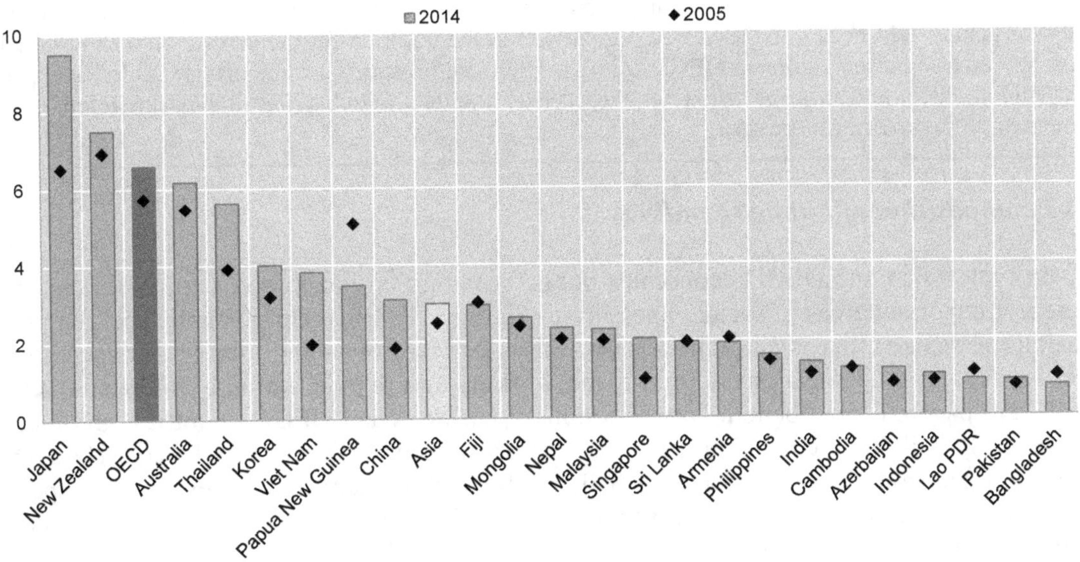

Source: World Health Organization; *OECD Health Database*.

StatLink *http://dx.doi.org/10.1787/888933457479*

Box 2.4. Public Health Insurance in Indonesia

Indonesia's public health care programme targeted at the poor Jamkesmas (Jaminan Kesehatan Masyarakat), was fully financed by central government and administered by the Ministry of Health (MoH). The programme guaranteed access to health facilities, including Public Health Care Centres, which provide primary level of care services as well as referral services to both public and private hospitals. However, the poor households' utilisation of Jamkesmas was low since the programme does not cover all costs of access the health care service, including the cost of transport, loss of salary or possible childcare coverage. Awareness among the poor population of Jamkesmas benefits was also lacking.

Indonesia is engaged in the process of implementing universal health-care coverage (UHC). The actual rollout started in 2014 and is projected to be finalised by 2019. In January 2014 various public schemes (including Jamkesmas) were unified in a single agency (BPJS Kesehatan) tasked with the implementation of the National Health Insurance Program (JKN). Initially, the programme covered about 120 million existing users of previous schemes – about half of the population – of which some 86 million ex-members of Jamkesmas.

The financing of this ambitious package is still unclear, which raises concerns as to UHC's sustainability. In 2015, the deficit of BPJS Kesehatan was IDR 4 trillion (around USD 300 million) for 162 million users and is forecast to reach nearly IDR 10 trillion in 2016, while the covered population could reach 186 million (Indonesia Investments, 2016).

Box 2.4. Public Health Insurance in Indonesia *(cont.)*

Public investments is also need to address the important health infrastructure gaps in Indonesia (e.g. the number of hospital beds per capita is extremely low by international standards), which are likely to increase as demand for services increases with improved living standards.

To have a sustainable UHC system, the government needs to adjust premiums to reflect costs and make sure that coverage increases equally across population layers. Health-care financing is ensured by premiums paid by the government for the poorest, while the rest of the population is divided into three classes according to their income, with recent increases in contribution rates for higher income groups. Ultimately, the finalisation of UHC and associated increased facilities is potentially a major risk for future public expenditure sustainability. Contribution rates and cost structures will need to be reviewed regularly, and the tradition for the private sector to provide health-care services should also be reinvigorated OECD, 2016f). There are prospects for the private sector to expand, given the growing middle class, and it is important for the private hospitals to subscribe to JKN in future, even though initial attempts to do so were not successful.

The composition of public spending

In both Asian and OECD economies public spending on health and senior citizens are the most important areas of social expenditure (Figure 2.8). On average, public spending on health and senior citizens accounts for two-thirds or more of public total social spending. Across Asia, public social spending on the working-age population and children is very low. Paid parental leave benefits are uncommon outside Asian OECD countries, and most of the early childhood education and care supports concern children aged 3 to 5 (OECD, 2014a). Exceptions are Armenia, Azerbaijan, China, Singapore and Mongolia that spent considerable amounts in terms of social support for the working age population and children often in the form of income/means-tested social assistance support or child benefits as in Mongolia (Box 2.5).

Public spending on pensions is particularly high in Japan (Figure 2.8, bottom panel), where senior citizens constitute 26% of the population (Figure 1.9). Furthermore, the earnings-related nature of its pension system contributes to public spending on old age and survivor spending amounting to 12% of GDP in 2013 (OECD, 2014a). Public outlays on pensions are considerably lower in Australia, Korea and New Zealand, where the elderly population is currently relatively small, while pension arrangements as "Superannuation" are considered as private social expenditures (Adema et al., 2011). In addition to considerable outlays on health and old-age and survivor pensions, OECD countries in the region also devote considerable public resources to active and passive employment supports (3% of GDP) and family cash benefits and services (2% of GDP).

Figure 2.8. Spending on health and elderly citizens are the two main areas of social protection

Public social expenditure by broad social policy area, as a percent of GDP, in 2013/14 or latest year available

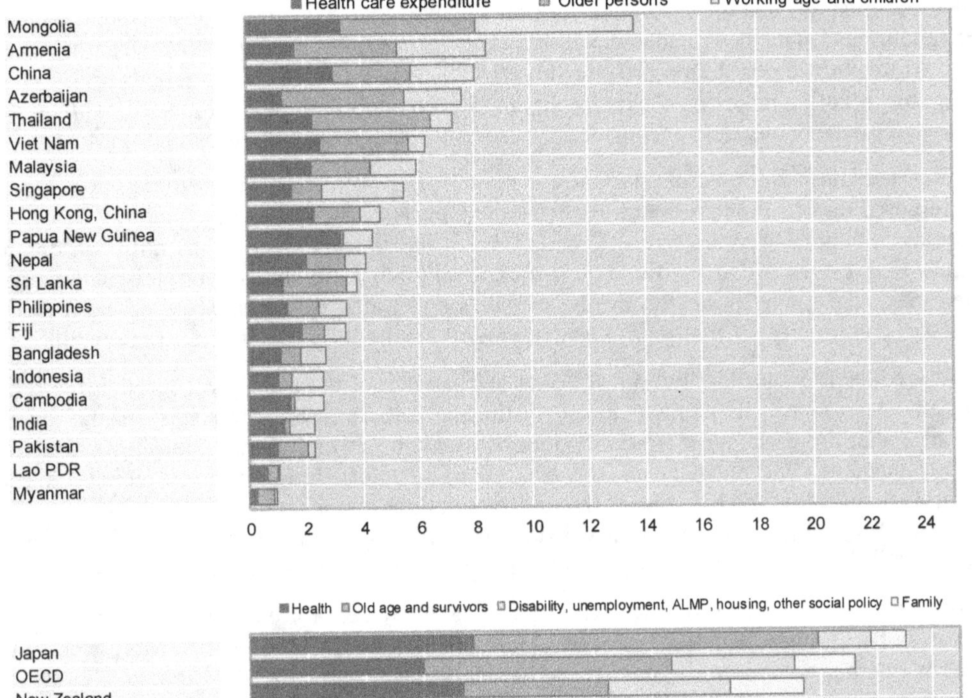

Source: ILO, *The World Social Protection Report 2014-15*, http://www.social-protection.org/gimi/gess/ShowTheme.action?th.themeId=3985, ADB staff estimates based on country reports Social Protection Indicator, 2015, Health from World Health Organisation Database (WHO), *OECD Social Expenditure Database*, (http://www.oecd.org/social/expenditure.htm).

StatLink *http://dx.doi.org/10.1787/888933457483*

Box 2.5. Mongolia's Child Money Programme

The Child Money Programme was launched in January 2005. Initially, the programme was a targeted conditional cash transfer. Families with three or more children under the age of 18 living under the minimum subsistence level received monthly cash allowances of MNT 3 000 (equivalent to USD 2.49 according to the 2005 exchange rate). From July 2006 until 1 January 2010 the programme was universal conditional on school enrolment. The programme was discontinued in 2010, but since 1 October 2012 the programme was reintroduced as a universal cash benefit without any conditionality paid at MNT 20 000 per child per month (Peyron-Bista et al., 2016).

In 2007, the Government of Mongolia established the Human Development Fund (HDF) in order to use revenues from the mining sector (mineral wealth) towards the economic and human development of the country, and the HDF finances the Child Money programme. In 2011, parliament stipulated a large allocation to all citizens (equivalent to 40% of the Central Government budget) to citizens for health insurance and student tuition fees. However, the IMF and World Bank criticised this use of the HDF as exceedingly expansionary and contributory to high inflation rates in 2011 and 2012 (ADB, 2016).

With rapidly rising budget deficits in the first half year of 2016, a newly elected government proposed budget cuts in August 2016 (World Bank, 2016), including a re-introduction of targeting of the Child Money Programme to about 60% of children (Peyron-Bista et al., 2016). The debate on this issue is likely to recur and could usefully be informed by international best practice and evaluations on the effectiveness of targeting mechanisms as one may be re-introduced.

Box 2.6. The Zakat system in Malaysia

Malaysia is a federal constitutional monarchy with the constitution declaring Islam as the official religion of the Federation whilst recognising freedom of religion for non-Muslims. Malaysia has a legal system which facilitates the co-existence of federal and state laws and the Syariah (*sharia*) law. According to the Department of Statistics of Malaysia (2011), 61.3% of the population are Muslims, 19.8% Buddhists, 9.2% Christians, 6.3% Hindus and other minorities. Given the Muslim majority, Zakat (donations) – being one of the pillars of faith in Islam – has an important role in Malaysian society, and is considered as a tool to help reduce poverty among Muslims.

Zakat is a religion-based tax which forms part of the main social protection programmes in Malaysia. Zakat is a mandatory levy imposed on Muslims collected by the state and private agencies and equal to 2.5% of assets over and above the minimum amount of wealth (*nisab*) to satisfy basic needs (this amount has not been defined in absolute terms). The funds thus raised are then distributed among eligible individuals who fall under one of the eight beneficiary categories such as the poor, the needy, refugees and Zakat officials. Most of the recipients of the aid belong to the Muslim community. In Malaysia, Zakat payments can be fully offset against tax liabilities.

The administration, collection and distribution of Zakat are handled at the state level through the religious council. Since the different states have their own Zakat institutions, there are differences in the interpretation and implementation of Zakat in each state (Hatta and Subramaniam, 2015). Figure 2.9 shows the trends in Zakat collection as a percentage of GDP in Malaysia (see also, OECD, 2016d). The significant increase in Zakat collection and redistribution over the years may be due to factors such as the increasing ease of making payments – with the introduction of online payment and monthly salary deductions, an increase in the efficiency of Zakat management, the privatisation of Zakat institutions in some states, and the increasing level of the income of Zakat payers.

The efficiency of Zakat institutions in Malaysia can be further improved, for example through the unification of the collection and distribution process at the national level (Abdulkader and Wahid, 2010). Moreover, Zakat institutions could co-ordinate with other government agencies – MAIMs, NGOs such as TEKUN and collaborate with the micro-finance institutions such as Amanah Ikhtiar Malaysia (AIM) to better redistribute funds. Linking the Zakat system with micro-finance institutions, would encourage investment in human capital development, education and skills development among the poor thereby fostering productive capacity building (Usman and Tasmin, 2016).

In theory, cash redistribution to the poor increases the purchasing power of those who have a relatively high propensity to consume and hence boosts consumption. However, the effect of Zakat on consumption stimulation in Malaysia appears to be limited (Suprayitno et al., 2013). This may be related to low payment rates and/ or the Zakat system covering only a part of the poor population.

Figure 2.9. Zakat collection in Malaysia amounts to 0.2% of GDP

Zakat collection in % of GDP

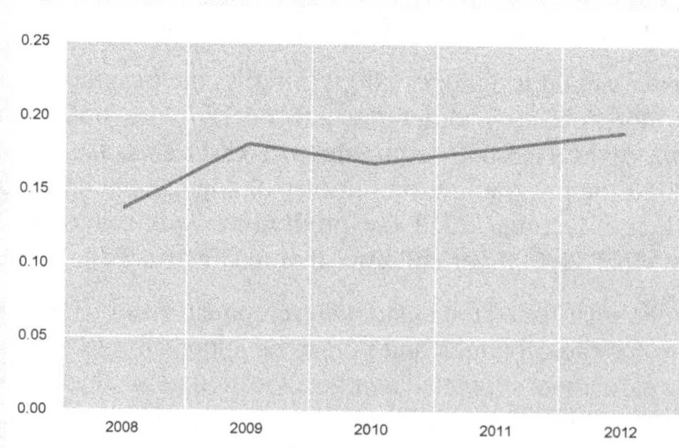

Source: Kajian Politik Untuk Perubahan, 2012 and World Development Indicators (The World Bank, 2016).

StatLink http://dx.doi.org/10.1787/888933457491

In Azerbaijan and China spending on supports for the working age population and children in 2012 was about 2% of GDP, which includes social assistance supports. In Azerbaijan, targeted social assistance was introduced in 2006 which the number of families receiving assistance tripling over the 2007-14 period to almost 145 000, but with the slump in oil prices and oil revenue the number of families receiving support fell to just below 100 000. In China, the number of social assistance recipients in 2015 amount to about 67 million (18 million in urban areas and 49 million in rural areas), and payment schedules seem to affect financial incentives to work for recipients, as in so many OECD countries (OECD, 2017, *forthcoming*). In some other countries including Malaysia social assistance payments can be supplemented by supports that often have a religious background (Box 2.6).

On average across the OECD, public social spending on cash benefits amounted to about 10% of GDP in 2014 of which about one-sixth concerns spending on benefits that are either income and/or means-tested (Figure 2.10). Thus, most social spending in the OECD concerns spending that derives from contributory records through social insurance schemes or universal categorical tax-financed benefits that are not subject to an income test (e.g. universal child benefits in many OECD countries). New Zealand, and in particular Australia, have public social protection systems that greatly rely on income-testing in delivering social support. By contrast social protection systems in both Japan and Korea rely heavily on social insurance principles in the provision of social benefits, and income-tested social assistance spending amounts to less than 1% of GDP.

Figure 2.10. Social transfers in Australia and New Zealand are more likely to be income-tested than in other OECD countries

Public spending on income and means-test benefits as a percent of public social spending on cash benefits (and GDP in brackets), 2013/14 or latest year available

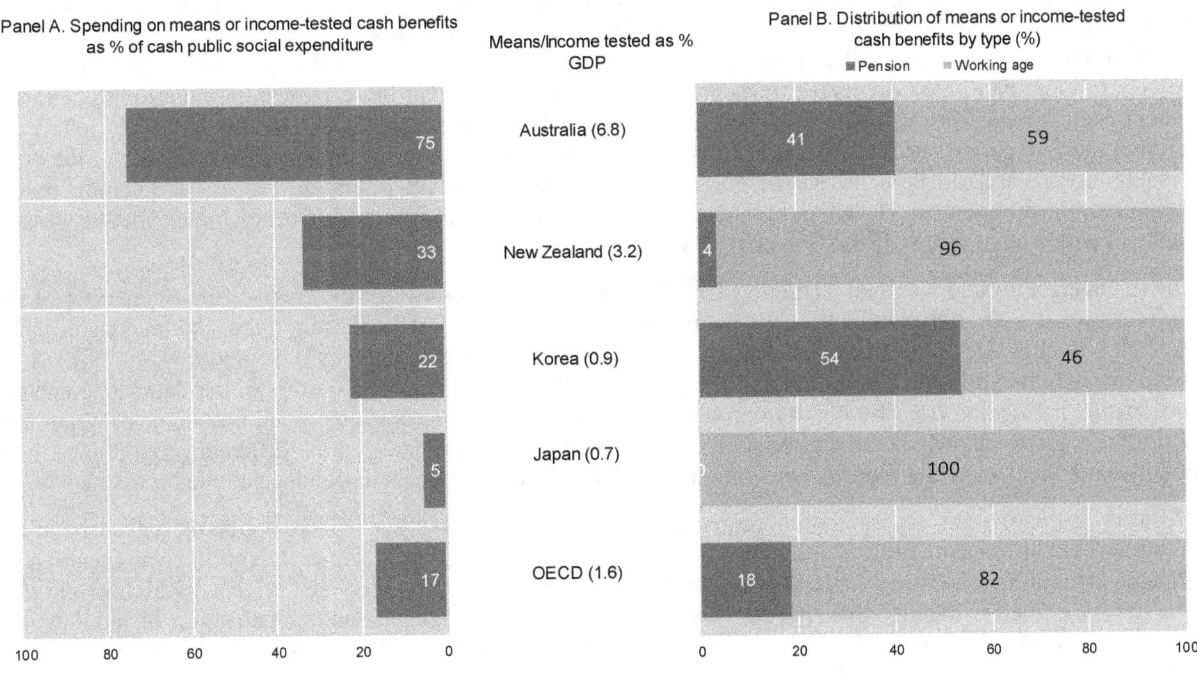

Source: OECD Social Expenditure Database (http://www.oecd.org/social/expenditure.htm).

StatLink http://dx.doi.org/10.1787/888933457506

The effectiveness of social protection systems in fighting poverty in OECD countries depends on spending levels, the degree of effective targeting at low income households (see Box 2.7), but also the level of taxation and the extent to which richer households pay proportionally more tax than households at the lower end of the income distribution are taxed (Adema et al., 2014).

In most Asian countries the effectives of social spending in fighting poverty or improving health across the population is determined by spending levels rather than the nature of tax system, as the income tax base is limited. And the relationship is as can be expected: Figure 2.11 illustrates that countries with higher public social expenditure tend to be those with lower absolute poverty rates, and countries with higher public expenditure on health – which tend to be the more advanced economies in the region – have the highest life expectancy.

Box 2.7. Indonesia's Unified Database (UDB)

In the aftermath of the 1998 financial crisis, Indonesia introduced various poverty alleviating programmes, most of which became part of the social safety net afterwards. The main household-based programmes that were introduced were: the Rice for the Poor programme (Raskin), Cash Transfers for Poor Students (BSM), public health insurance (JKN) and the Conditional Cash Transfer programme for Poor Families (PKH).

The 2005 socio-economic population survey (PSE 2005) and the 2008 Data collection for Social Protection Programmes Survey (PPLS) were conducted to identify the beneficiaries of some of the programmes. However, these targeting approaches were limited due to the heavy dependence on local level officials and service providers, leading to inclusion and exclusion errors: some non-poor households were included while some poor households were excluded. Furthermore, despite having similar target groups, there was little similarity in selection mechanisms of the different programmes. In order to overcome these difficulties, the Government of Indonesia established a unified registry – the Unified Database – to identify beneficiaries of the different social assistance programmes.

Indonesia's Unified Database (UDB) is an electronic data system which consists of detailed socio-economic information and welfare status of 24.5 million households (96 million individuals), mostly derived from the 2011 PPLS. Poverty indicators from the PPLS have been carefully selected so as to limit the risk that respondents tailor their answers to what they think may give them the largest benefit. Based on these indicators, households with the lowest socio-economic conditions were identified using Proxy-Means Testing (PMT). Households in the UDB are classified into the four poorest deciles, which can further be divided into percentiles, ranging from the 5th to the 40th. The nationally comparable decile or percentile classification in the UDB gives policy developers and administrators of social protection programmes (UDB users) the flexibility to design and implement programmes for the desired coverage level within available budgets (Bah et al., 2015).

The UDB is managed by the National Targeting Unit for Poverty Reduction (UPSPK) part of the Secretariat of the National Team for the Acceleration of Poverty Reduction (TNP2K), which falls directly under the responsibility of the President of the Republic of Indonesia (http://www.tnp2k.go.id/en/about-tnp2k/structure-of-tnp2k/). It is responsible for dissemination of information and the provision of technical support to users of the database, with the aim of optimising its use and contributing to improving the effectiveness of the various social assistance programmes. Using a single source to identify beneficiaries enables better synchronisation between the different programmes, both at the national and local level and reduces duplication of the identification process and reduce administrative costs.

The UDB aims to improve the accuracy of its targeting and achieve high coverage. Since, not being registered in the database implies exclusion from most of the social protection programmes, prospective recipients have an incentive to do so. Raising awareness of existing supports and introducing a well-functioning feedback system – which would also help potential beneficiaries identify their needs – would improve the maintenance and actualisation of the database which is key to its effectiveness (Bah et al., 2015). Ultimately, the system could evolve into a rights-based social protection system that provides social benefits where they are needed.

Figure 2.11. Increase public social and health spending are associated with less poverty and longer lives

Panel A. Public social expenditure and poverty rate

Panel B. Health expenditure and life expectancy

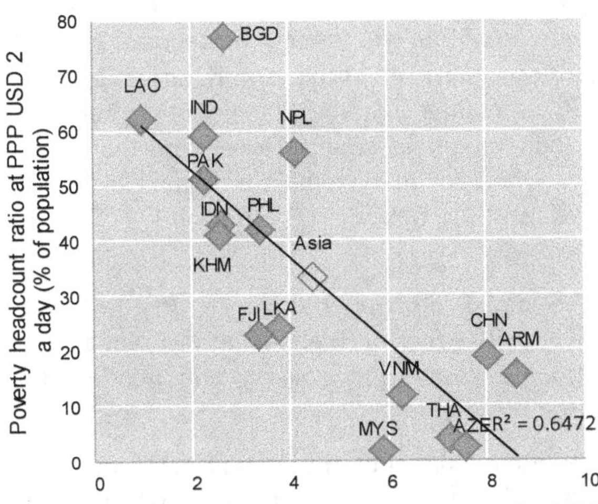

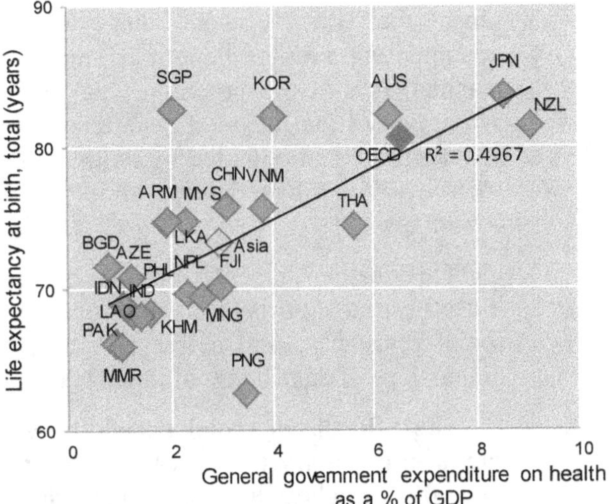

Source: World Bank, World Development Indicators, http://databank.worldbank.org/data/reports.aspx?source=world-development-indicators, as in August 2015. ILO, *The World Social Protection Report 2014-15*, http://www.social-protection.org/gimi/gess/ShowTheme.action?th.themeId=3985, ADB staff estimates based on country reports Social Protection Indicator, 2016, World Health Organisation Database (WHO), OECD (2016), *Social Expenditure Database*, (www.oecd.org/social/expenditure.htm).

StatLink ᐧ http://dx.doi.org/10.1787/888933457513

2.4. The ADB Social Protection Indicator[2]

For the assessment of social protection policy and its role in poverty reduction, also in developing countries, the ADB developed a Social Protection Indicator as a tool for analysis. Its development was driven by the ADBs social protection strategy and key questions such as how much is spent on social protection in any given country, what are the programmes, who is covered and how can the implementation of social protection programmes be monitored (ADB, 2006, 2013 and 2016). These issues are also pertinent to the OECD Social Expenditure (SOCX) and Social Recipients (SOCR) Databases (OECD, 2016a and 2016g), and the scope of the underlying data for both is compatible although there are differences. As a rule of thumb, social spending totals calculated in line with the ADB methodology (as below) are likely to be a little lower than OECD data as the ADB data do not capture all public health spending for all countries – the SPI does not account for free universal public health services financed out of general taxation – and does not account for the impact of tax systems on social spending (Adema et al., 2011). The latter may not be that much of an issue in many Asian countries, but tax systems often have a large effect on social spending in OECD countries and play a key role in the redistribution of social support in OECD tax/benefit systems (see, for example, Adema et al., 2014; and OECD, 2011a and 2015a).

The ADB Social Protection Indicator (SPI) is unique in that it tries to encapsulate information on social spending and recipients in one single number to illustrate the extent of social support in a country and give an indication on to what extent social protection reaches the intended beneficiaries, e.g. the poor, the elderly or the unemployed. In that sense, the SPI gauges a country's "efficiency" in spending on social protection by documenting average benefit payments as well as how many intended beneficiaries are reached. It is also a potential weak spot of the SPI as results become dependent on the estimation of the intended beneficiaries as done by consultants at country level, and these problems are compounded by double counting issues when social systems are organised in such a way that beneficiaries simultaneously receive multiple benefits (as often in OECD countries).

This section presents information on the ADB Social Protection Indicator (SPI), and illustrates the importance of different components of social spending (e.g., social insurance, social assistance, and active labour market programmes); and the poverty and gender dimensions of distributional impacts of social spending.

The SPI relates social expenditures to the total intended beneficiaries and GDP per capita in a country (Box 2.8) and results indicate that SPI increases with national wealth. The SPI is highest in Japan where the ratio of expenditures to intended beneficiaries is approximately 11.7% of GDP per capita, while the SPI is only just above 1% in low-income countries as Bangladesh and Cambodia (Table 2.3).

However, some countries score noticeably above or below the average of countries with similar levels of income. For example, the SPI for Azerbaijan, Armenia, Mongolia and Viet Nam is well above the average for countries with similar levels of income, while there are various countries (including India, Indonesia, Lao PDR and Papua New Guinea) where the SPI is lower than what might be expected on basis of average wealth levels. In these countries large proportions of the population living rural areas and engaged in informal employment outside any statutory or collective system of social protection. In these countries the traditional reliance on family and community support remains as important as ever (Thompson, 2002).

Box 2.8. The ADB Social Protection Indicator

ADB (2016) calculates the Social Protection Indicator (SPI) involving data on pubic social protection expenditure and (potential) beneficiaries for 2012. The SPI is defined to encompass three broad areas: i) social insurance (e.g., contributory scheme that reduce risks associated with old age, disability, unemployment, sickness, etc.); ii) social assistance (e.g., non-contributory cash or in-kind transfers and welfare services); and iii) labour market programmes that actively help people secure employment through employment services, skill development and training or special work programmes). The data for the SPI was mainly gathered from government statistics and reports by international financial institutions and bilateral agencies, discussions and interviews with agencies responsible for social protection programmes, and household survey data. The disaggregation of social protection beneficiaries and expenditures by poverty and gender are only indicative and based on either i) approximation from the implementing agencies, ii) indication from household surveys or iii) professional judgments (experts' opinion) of the country data compilers.

The Social Protection Indicator (SPI) is defined as the ratio of public social spending to all intended or "potential" beneficiaries in each country, as divided by GDP per capita of the country:

$$SPI = \frac{\left[\frac{\sum E}{\sum PB}\right]}{Z}, \text{ where } E \text{ represents social expenditure; } PB \text{ represents potential or intended social beneficiaries; and}$$
$$Z \text{ represents GDP per capita.}$$

The SPI can be used to consider the "breadth" and "depth" of coverage of social protection, where the breadth refers to the ratio of actual beneficiaries to intended or potential beneficiaries of social protection, and the depth is defined as the average expenditures per actual beneficiary, divided by GDP per capita:

$$D = \frac{\left[\frac{\sum E}{\sum AB}\right]}{Z}, \text{ where } D \text{ represents depth; } E \text{ represents social expenditures, and } Z \text{ represents the GDP per capita.}$$

$$B = \frac{\sum AB}{\sum PB}, \text{ where } B \text{ denotes breadth; } AB \text{ represents actual social beneficiaries; and, PB represents potential or}$$
$$\text{intended social beneficiaries.}$$

The SPI can also be calculated for components of social expenditure. For example ADB (2016), considers a three-way disaggregation of social spending: social insurance (including items as pension and health insurance), social assistance (assistance to the elderly, health assistance, and poverty alleviation programmes, and labour market programmes). Similarly, the SPI could be disaggregated in social spending towards the "poor" or the "non-poor" or towards men and women.

In that case each of the SPI components is expressed as a ratio of total expenditures on that component divided by the corresponding total of potential beneficiaries of that component. However, for the SPIs for the different components to add up to the overall SPI, they have to be multiplied by their corresponding "population weight", which is the ratio of potential beneficiaries for that component to all potential beneficiaries of all social protection.

For example, when the SPI is disaggregated in social support to poor and non-poor potential beneficiaries, the SPI_p is based on the sum of all expenditures on the poor divided by all the poor (since the poor in their entirety are regarded as the potential beneficiaries). But it is weighted by the ratio of all the poor to all potential beneficiaries of social protection:

$$SPI_p = \left[\frac{\sum E_p}{\sum PB_p}\right] \times \left[\frac{\sum PB_p}{\sum PB}\right]$$

Similarly, for social spending on the "non-poor". SPI_{np} is the sum of all expenditures on total non-poor potential beneficiaries multiplied by the weight of the ratio of all non-poor potential beneficiaries divided by all potential beneficiaries of social protection:

$$SPI_{np} = \left[\frac{\sum E_{np}}{\sum PB_{np}}\right] \times \left[\frac{\sum PB_{np}}{\sum PB}\right]$$

Both SPI_p and SPI_{np} have to be divided by GDP per capita in order to assure that $SPI_p + SPI_{np} = SPI$.

Table 2.3. The social protection indicator is generally higher in richer countries

The social protection indicator (SPI) and GDP per capita, by income group, Asia and the Pacific, 2012

	SPI (%)	GDP per capita (USD)
High income countries[1,2]	**7.7**	**41 018**
Japan	11.7	46 549
Singapore	6.3	52 052
Korea	5.1	24 454
Upper-middle income countries [1,2]	**3.1**	**8 089**
Azerbaijan	6.2	7 500
China	4.3	6 093
Malaysia	4.2	10 324
Thailand	2.9	5 913
Fiji	1.3	3 668
Lower-middle income countries[1,2]	**2.8**	**2 357**
Armenia	4.9	3 293
Mongolia	4.8	3 617
Viet Nam	4	1 755
Sri Lanka	2.7	2 930
Philippines	2.2	2 613
Pakistan	1.4	1 150
India	1.3	1 555
Indonesia	1.2	3 552
Lao PDR	0.6	1 394
Papua New Guinea	0.1	2 152
Low income countries[1,2]	**1.1**	**833**
Nepal	1.7	664
Cambodia	1.2	971
Bangladesh	1.1	740
Overall ADB average[1]	**3.1**	**6 908**

1. The able includes information on the 25 countries for which data when available is presented. However, the ADB calculations concerns 38 countries in Asia and the Pacific, and results for all these countries are used to calculate the unweighted "overall ADB average". The table includes information for all **high income countries** for which data is available. However, the average for **upper-middle income countries** concerns results for Azerbaijan, China, the Cook Islands, Fiji, Malaysia, the Maldives, the Marshall Islands, Nauru, Palau, Thailand and Tonga; the average for **lower-middle income countries** concerns: Armenia, Bhutan, Georgia, India, Indonesia, Kiribati, the Kyrgyz Republic, Lao PDR, Mongolia, Micronesia, Pakistan, Papua New Guinea, the Philippines, Samoa, the Solomon Islands, Sri Lanka, Timor-Leste, Uzbekistan, Vanuatu and Viet Nam; and the average SPI score for **low-income countries** is based on results for Bangladesh, Cambodia, Nepal and Tajikistan.

2. Low-, middle- and high-income countries are defined in line with World Bank definitions, see http://data.worldbank.org/about/country-classifications.

Source: ADB Staff estimates based on country reports, see ADB (2016a).

StatLink ᠁᠍ http://dx.doi.org/10.1787/888933457584

Breadth and depth of social protection

The SPI can be used to consider the "breadth" and "depth" of social protection, where the breadth refers to the ratio of actual beneficiaries to intended or potential beneficiaries of social protection, and the depth is defined as the average expenditures per actual beneficiary, divided by GDP per capita.

To start with the latter, across country groupings by income, on average there does not appear to be a dramatic difference in social spending per *actual* beneficiary. In middle-and high income around spending per beneficiary was about 8.5 % of GDP per capita in 2012.

In low-income countries, spending per actual beneficiary was considerably lower at on average 5.5% of GDP per capita (Figure 2.13).

Spending per beneficiary is particularly high among social insurance recipients. Among middle-income countries spending per beneficiary is particularly high in Armenia, Azerbaijan and particularly Uzbekistan where the average pension payment is close to average GDP per capita (ADB, 2016). These countries have inherited their pension systems from the former USSR which they have to reconsider in terms of eligibility criteria, retirement ages, and the linkage between contribution rates and benefit payments in order to safeguard the financial sustainability of their pension systems.

Average spending per beneficiary is more balanced in high income countries where the depth of coverage for both social insurance and social assistance was equivalent to about 9 to 10% of GDP per capita in 2012. This balance is desirable as different segments of the population tend to benefit from different forms of social protection. This balance is lacking among low-income countries, where, spending per recipients of a social insurance benefits is very high at over 60% of GDP per capita. This ratio is highest in Bangladesh where spending on pensions amounted to around twice the level of GDP per capita in 2012. This is because there were less than 400 000 pension beneficiaries on an elderly population of about 10 million (ADB, 2016).

The Bangladesh example is an extreme case illustrating a general trend: the proportion of intended beneficiaries that receive support decreases with national per capital income. Figure 2.12 shows that on average in high-income countries just over 90% of the potential beneficiaries are covered by social support, mostly by social insurance benefits. In middle income countries about 50 to 70% of the intended beneficiaries are reached, with an increasing role for social assistance rather than social insurance benefits. In low-income countries, only a quarter of the intended benefit population is covered and on average less than 5% of the intended beneficiaries are covered by social insurance benefits.

Labour market programmes play a modest role in social protection in Asia: spending on and coverage of labour market policies is generally limited across Asia (Figure 2.12). There are two major types: i) skills development and training, and ii) cash-or food-for-work programmes. ADB (2016) suggests, that spending on cash for work programmes is three times as high as on skills development and training programmes, and that the cash for work programmes (as in Bangladesh and India) also reach a much larger number of beneficiaries. However, cash for work programmes do not improve skills and in themselves do not offer opportunities to participants to escape poverty. The challenge is to improve these programmes so that they contribute to the transition to more productive employment, and more and better jobs.

Figure 2.12. Unlike the "breadth" of social spending its "depth" does not appear to be strongly related to income across countries

Panel A. "Depth" is defined as the average expenditures per actual beneficiary, divided by GDP per capita, 2012

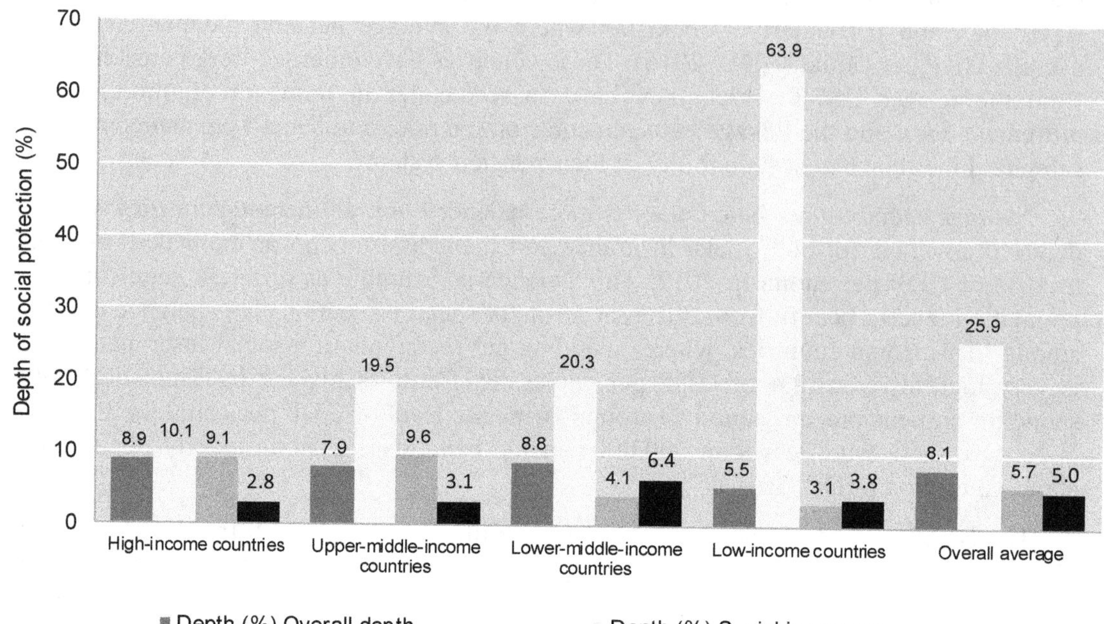

Panel B. "Breadth" is defined as the ratio of actual beneficiaries to intended or potential beneficiaries of social protection, 2012

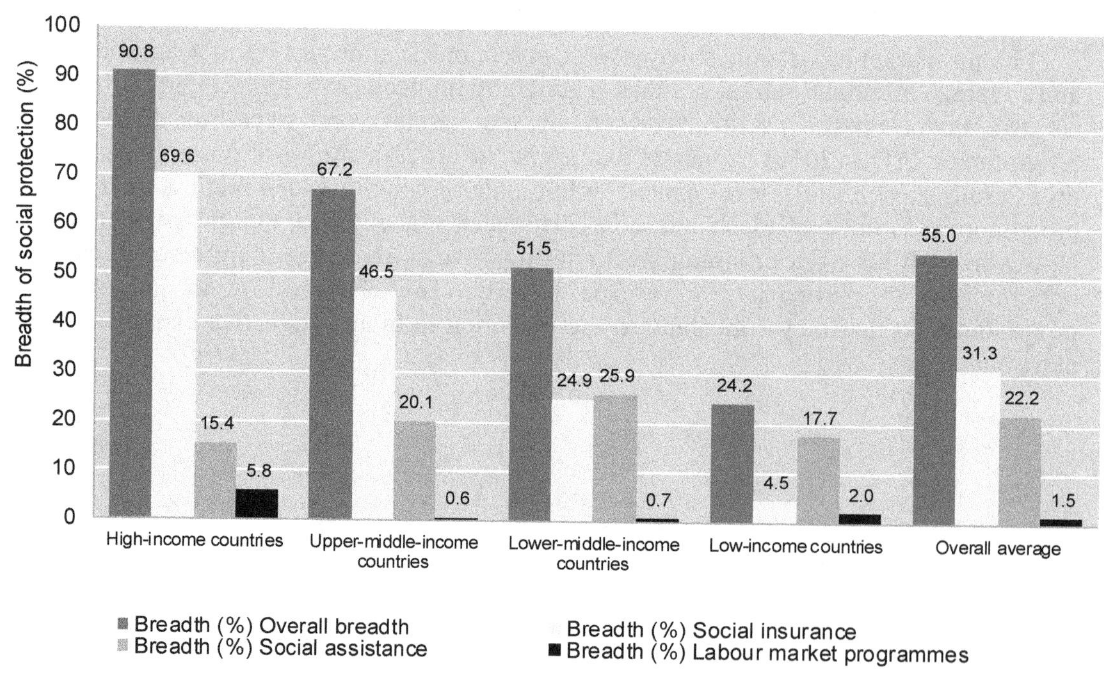

Source: ADB (2016), Social Protection Indicator.

StatLink ᵐˢᵖ *http://dx.doi.org/10.1787/888933457520*

Poverty and gender dimensions

The SPI as a ratio of social spending to intended beneficiaries provides an indication on the distributional impact of social expenditure, as it helps to gauge how much support the poor receive compared to the non-poor.

Across, countries with different average standards of living, the SPIs for the poor are generally significantly smaller than the SPIs for the non-poor (Figure 2.13). Overall, the SPI for the poor is only equivalent to 0.9% of GDP per capita, whereas the SPI for the non-poor is equivalent to 2.8% of GDP per capita. Across income groups the non-poor benefit disproportionally form access to social insurance benefits which to a large extend reflects the weight of pension expenditures to former formal sector workers. By contrast, the poor benefit much more from social assistance, but payment rates of and overall spending on social assistance are much lower than for earnings-related insurance benefits.

Across countries with different living standards there are differences in the inequality of distribution of support to the poor and non-poor. The SPI to the poor is about half of that to the non-poor in both low and high income countries. In low income countries, this is because the average SPI for everyone is quite low, while in high income countries there is considerable spending on social assistance benefits (and to a lesser extent labour market supports – to which the poor have access.

However, the outcomes for upper middle-income countries are much more inequitable, with the SPI for the non-poor being six times higher as the SPI for the poor. This is mostly attributable to a large difference in access between the non-poor and the poor to social insurance benefits. All this clearly suggests that a key challenge in social protection policy is to enable the poor to gain access to formal employment and its associated benefits (Chapter 1).

The SPIs for men and women are closer to each other than those for the poor and non-poor (Figure 2.13, Panel B). With the SPI disaggregation being dependent on population weights (Box 2.6), this is also related to proportions of men and women in the population being more similar than those of the poor and non-poor.

Figure 2.13, Panel B shows, that the SPI for women is equivalent to 1.6% of GDP per capita compared with 2.1% of GDP per capita for men. Furthermore, the difference is entirely due to the difference in access to social insurance benefits. In turn, this is related to gender gaps in employment and labour force participation in favour of men, while women are also under-represented among formal sector workers (Chapter 1). Gender differences often concern pensions with men more likely to draw a pension than women. Women tend to live longer than men, and they may receive a survivor's pension when the retired husband passes on, however, this effect does not outweigh the overall initial spending focus of social insurance benefits on men. Also, maternity benefits are paid to women, but as coverage is limited in Asia spending is small and does not significantly redress the gender imbalance in social insurance spending.

Figure 2.13. Social protection in Asia reaches the non-poor rather than the poor and men more than women

Panel A. Social protection indicator by poverty status and income group, Asia, 2012

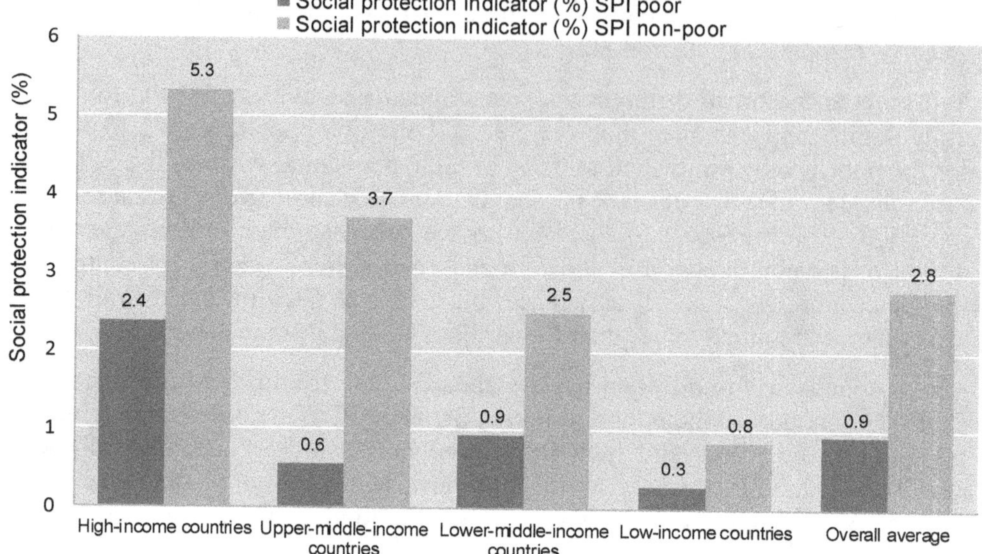

Panel B. Social protection indicator by gender, Asia, 2012

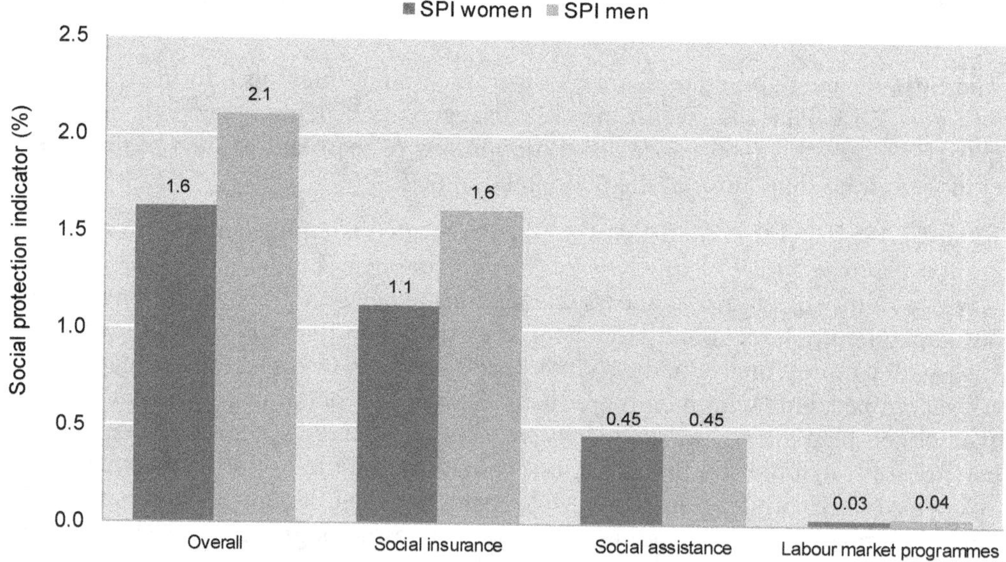

Note: Administrative data on distributional outcomes between poor and non-poor and men and women are usually not available, the national consultants who gathered the data had to rely on estimates by government officials and other experts, or derive estimates from other sources such as censuses, labour force surveys, and household income and expenditure surveys (see ADB, 2016). Therefore, these results should be considered as indicative rather than definitive.

Source ADB (2016), Social Protection Indicator.

StatLink ᵐˢᵖ *http://dx.doi.org/10.1787/888933457530*

2.5.   Concluding remarks

Public social expenditure in Asia is increasing, but remains low compared to OECD countries at 5% of GDP. The major outlays are on pensions and health, and most of the relevant social insurance type benefits are tied to formal employment, and as such are more likely to benefit non-poor households rather than poor ones and men rather than women. Social assistance benefits may be available to the poorest households, especially if these are well targeted. However, the intensity of social assistance support may not be enough to lift households out of poverty, and many vulnerable low-income families receive very few, if any, social protection benefits.

There is a growing role for non-contributory type old age allowances and some Asian countries have established non-contributory pension schemes with widespread coverage, as the main and sometimes only system of income provision in retirement. Chinas has been most successful in extending coverage of social insurance programmes, but many other economies find it very difficult to effectively increase coverage: the administrative capacity is often lacking to register participants in insurance schemes and/or collect contributions from employers and employees.

Spending share on social assistance are generally low, and spending on labour market programmes is even lower, with many low and middle income countries not having a functional unemployment compensation scheme. To some extent such low expenditures are linked to strong economic growth, but the low spending levels also raise concerns on the adequacy of supports.

Extending social assistance and social insurance schemes is needed to reduce poverty and provide for the increasing medical and income needs of ageing populations increase. Investment in children, whether or not by means of conditional cash transfers, and associated health and early and primary education services is key. Greater investment in active labour market programmes would provide informal workers and the poor and vulnerable population with greater access to employment guarantee schemes or skill development and training.

But the success of extending coverage of social insurance and other contributory schemes would ultimately rely on the ability of countries to expand productive, formal employment. The increase in average income in Asia has increased the scope for increasing public revenues, whereas the administrative capacity to effectively introduce and operate a contributory system of social support which provides opportunities to give large groups of the populations access to forms of social protection that are tied to employment.

Notes

1. The OECD Social Expenditure Database (SOCX, www.oecd.org/social/expenditure) has been designed to be compatible with the System of National Accounts and inter alia the System of Health Accounts (OECD/WHO/Eurostat, 2011; and European Commission, International Monetary Fund, OECD, United Nations and the World Bank, 2009). It is also broadly compatible – in the sense that individual expenditure items can be reclassified across different spending categories or functions – with the ADB's Social Protection Index (ADB, 2006 and 2013 and http://spi.adb.org/spidmz/index.jsp), and the ILO Social Security Inquiry – SSI (ILO, 2005 and www.ilo.org/dyn/ilossi/ssimain.home). In terms of social domain, the OECD has arguably the largest scope the different datasets as it has developed a methodology, which facilitates the comprehensive accounting of fiscal measures that affect social protection. See Adema et al. (2011) for a detailed methodological discussion and the OECD Social Expenditure webpages for the most recent data: http://www.oecd.org/els/soc/expenditure.htm).

2. This section was originally drafted by Sri Wening Handayani and her team at the Asian Development Bank, Manila The views expressed in this publication are those of the author and do not necessarily reflect the views and policies of the Asian Development Bank (ADB), its Board of Governors, or the governments they represent.

References

Abdulkader, R. and H. Wahid (2010), "Localization of Malaysian Zakah Distribution, Perceptions of Amil and Zakah Recipients", Paper presented at the seventh International Conference-The Tawhidi Epistemology: Zakah and waqf economy, Bangi.

ADB (2016*), The Social Protection Indicator, Assessing Results for Asia*, Asian Development Bank, Manila.

ADB (2013), The Social Protection Index: Assessing Results for Asia and the Pacific, Asian Development Bank, Manila, Philippines, http://www.adb.org/sites/default/files/pub/2013/social-protection-index.pdf.

ADB (2012), Social Protection for Older Persons – Social Pensions in Asia, Asian Development Bank, Manila, Philippines.

ADB (2006), Social Protection Index – for Committed Poverty Reduction, Asian Development Bank, Manila, Philippines.

Adema, W., P. Fron and M. Ladaique (2014), "How Much Do OECD Countries Spend on Social Protection and How Redistributive Are their Tax/benefit Systems", *International Social Security Review*, Vol. 67, No. 1/2014, pp. 1-25.

Adema, W., P. Fron and M. Ladaique (2011), "Is the European Welfare State Really More Expensive? Indicators on Social Spending, 1980-2012; and a Manual to the OECD Social Expenditure Database (SOCX)", *OECD Social, Employment and Migration Working Papers*, No. 124, OECD Publishing, Paris, http://dx.doi.org/10.1787/5kg2d2d4pbf0-en.

Bah, A., S. Nazara, and E. Satriawan (2015), "Indonesia's Single Registry for Social Protection Programmes", No. 49, International Policy Centre for Inclusive Growth.

Barrientos, A. (2013), *Social Assistance in Developing Countries*, Cambridge University Press.

DOSM (2011), "Population Distribution and Basic Demographic Characteristics Report 2010", Department of Statistics Malaysia, Kuala Lumpur.

DOSS (2015), *Year Book of Statistics Singapore 2015*, Department of Statistics, Ministry of Trade and Industry, Republic of Singapore.

European Commission, International Monetary Fund, OECD, United Nations and the World Bank (2009), *System of National Accounts 2008*, EC, IMF, OECD, UN and the World Bank, New York, http://unstats.un.org/unsd/nationalaccount/docs/SNA2008.pdf.

Eurostat (2012), *ESSPROS Manual and User Guidelines – 2012 Edition*, EUROSTAT, Luxembourg.

Hatta, Z. and J. Subramaniam (2015), "Social Expenditures of Malaysia for the period 2008-2012", OECD/Korea Policy Centre – Health and Social Policy Programme SOCX Technical Papers.

HelpAge International (2015), "Pension Watch: Social Protection in Older Age", Database available at: http://www.pension-watch.net/.

ILO (2016a), *Word Employment and Social Outlook: Trends 2016*, International Labour Office, Geneva.

ILO (2015a), "NORMLEX: Information System on International Labour Standards", Available online at http://www.ilo.org/dyn/normlex/en/ (March 2015).

ILO (2015b), *The State of Social Protection in ASEAN at the Dawn of Integration*, International Labour Organization, Bangkok

ILO (2015c), *World Employment and Social Outlook: The Changing Nature of Jobs*, International Labour Office, Geneva.

ILO (2014), World Social Protection Report 2014/2015: Building economic recovery, inclusive development and social justice, International Labour Office, Geneva.

ILO (2005), "ILO Social Security Inquiry", First Inquiry 2005, Manual, International Labour Office, Geneva, http://www.ilo.org/public/english/protection/secsoc/downloads/stat/ssimane.pdf.

Indonesia Investments (2016), "Indonesia's National Health Insurance Program: Rising Financial Mismatch", 3 March, http://www.indonesia-investments.com/news/todays-headlines/indonesia-s-nationalhealth-insurance-program-rising-financial-mismatch/item6563.

Mendes, P. (2009), "An Australian Perspective on Singaporean Welfare Policy, Social Work and Policy", *online journal*, Vol. 7, No. 1.

MHLW (2015), "Comprehensive Survey of Living Conditions", Ministry of Health, Labour and Welfare, Tokyo.

MOEL (2016), "Employment Insurance White Paper 2015", Ministry of Employment and Labour, Sejong-si, Korea.

MOEL (2010), "Employment Insurance White Paper 2009", Ministry of Employment and Labour, Seoul, Korea.

OECD (2017), *OECD Economic Surveys: China 2015*, OECD Publishing, Paris, http://dx.doi.org/10.1787/eco_surveys-chn-2017-en, forthcoming.

OECD (2016a), "The OECD Social Expenditure Database (SOCX), October 2016 Social Expenditure Update", OECD, Paris, http://www.oecd.org/els/soc/expenditure.htm.

OECD (2016b), *OECD Economic Surveys: Korea 2016*, OECD Publishing, Paris, http://dx.doi.org/10.1787/eco_surveys-kor-2016-en.

OECD (2016c), *OECD Revenue Statistics in Asian Countries 2016*, OECD Publishing, Paris, http://dx.doi.org/10.1787/9789264266483-en.

OECD (2016d), *OECD Revenue Statistics 2016*, OECD Publishing, Paris, http://dx.doi.org/10.1787/rev_stats-2016-en-fr.

OECD (2016e), *Health at a Glance Asia/Pacific*, OECD Publishing, Paris, http://dx.doi.org/10.1787/health_glance_ap-2016-en.

OECD (2016f), *OECD Economic Surveys: Indonesia 2016*, OECD Publishing, Paris, http://dx.doi.org/10.1787/eco_surveys-idn-2016-en.

OECD (2016g), *OECD Economic Surveys: Malaysia 2016*, OECD Publishing, Paris, http://dx.doi.org/10.1787/eco_surveys-mys-2016-en.

OECD (2016h), "The OECD Social Benefit Recipients Database (SOCR)", OECD, Paris, http://www.oecd.org/els/soc/recipients.htm.

OECD (2015a), *In It Together: Why Less Inequality Benefits All*, OECD Publishing, Paris, http://dx.doi.org/10.1787/9789264235120-en.

OECD (2015b), *Pensions at a Glance*, OECD Publishing, Paris, http://dx.doi.org/10.1787/pension_glance-2015-en.

OECD (2014), *Society at a Glance Asia/Pacific*, OECD Publishing, Paris, http://dx.doi.org/10.1787/9789264220553-en.

OECD (2013), *Pension at a Glance Asia/Pacific*, OECD Publishing, Paris, http://dx.doi.org/10.1787/pension_asia-2013-en.

OECD (2011), *Divided We Stand: Why Inequality Keeps Rising*, OECD Publishing, Paris, http://dx.doi.org/10.1787/9789264119536-en.

OECD/WHO/Eurostat (2011), *A System of Health Accounts: 2011 Edition*, OECD Publishing, Paris, http://dx.doi.org/10.1787/9789264116016-en.

Peyron-Bista, C., L. Amagalan and E. Nasan-Ulzi (2016), "The Universal Child Money Programme in Mongolia", Universal Social Protection Brief, http://www.ilo.org/wcmsp5/groups/public/---asia/---ro-bangkok/---ilo-beijing/documents/publication/wcms_534930.pdf.

Queisser, M., A. Reilly and Y. Hu (2016), "China's Pension System and Reform – An OECD perspective", *Economic and Political Studies*, Vol. 4, Special Issue: Ageing and Its Implications: China and the world, pp. 345-367, http://dx.doi.org/10.1080/20954816.2016.1251134.

Salditt, F., P. Whiteford and W. Adema (2008), "Pension Reform in China", *International Social Security Review*, Vol. 61, No. 3, pp. 47-71.

Sharma, S.K., ADB (2014), "Singapore: Updating and Improving Social Protection Index", Technical Assistance Consultant's Report, Asian Development Bank, Manila.

Suprayitno, E., R.A. Kader and A. Harun (2013), "The Impact of Zakat on Aggregate Consumption in Malaysia", *Journal of Islamic Economics, Banking and Finance*, Vol. 9, No. 1, pp. 39-62.

Thompson, K. (2002), "Social Protection in Southeast and East Asia", Friedrich-Ebert-Stiftung – Bonn, http://library.fes.de/pdf-files/iez/01443004.pdf.

U.S. SSA (2015), "Social Security Programs Throughout the World: Asia and the Pacific 2014", United States Social Security Administration, Washington DC.

Usman, A.S. and R. Tasmin (2016), "The Role of Islamic Micro-finance in Enhancing Human Development in Muslim Countries", *Journal of Islamic Finance*, Vol. 5, No. 1, pp. 53-62.

WHO (2016), "Data on Life Expectancy at Birth", retrieved on 10 October from: http://gamapserver.who.int/gho/interactive_charts/mbd/life_expectancy/atlas.html, World Health Organization, Geneva.

World Bank (2016), "Mongolia Economic Brief", September 2016, http://pubdocs.worldbank.org/en/349831473147873084/pdf/Mongolia-Economic-Briefs-0916-final.pdf.

Yoo, K. and B. Choi (2014), "Evaluation of Durunuri Program", KDI FOCUS, Vol. 38, Korea Development Institute, Seoul, Korea.

Database references

OECD Social Expenditure Database, http://www.oecd.org/social/expenditure.htm.

OECD Health Database, https://www.oecd.org/health/health-data.htm

Annex 2.A1
Background data to Chapter 2

Figure 2.A1.1. Pension coverage and GDP per capita

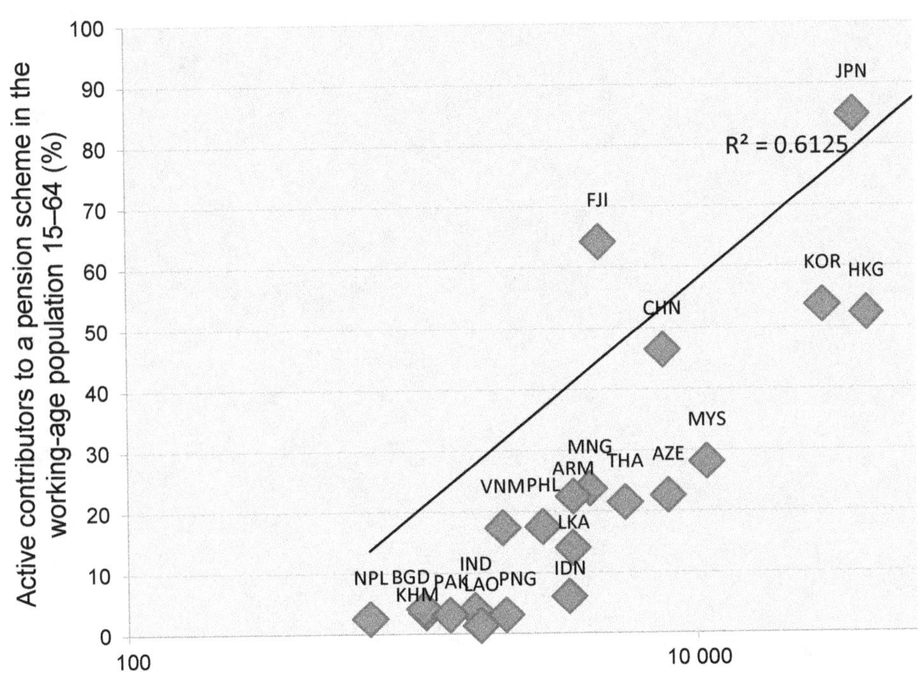

Source: ILO Social Protection Department database, World Bank development Indicators.

StatLink *http://dx.doi.org/10.1787/888933457543*

ORGANISATION FOR ECONOMIC CO-OPERATION
AND DEVELOPMENT

The OECD is a unique forum where governments work together to address the economic, social and environmental challenges of globalisation. The OECD is also at the forefront of efforts to understand and to help governments respond to new developments and concerns, such as corporate governance, the information economy and the challenges of an ageing population. The Organisation provides a setting where governments can compare policy experiences, seek answers to common problems, identify good practice and work to co-ordinate domestic and international policies.

The OECD member countries are: Australia, Austria, Belgium, Canada, Chile, the Czech Republic, Denmark, Estonia, Finland, France, Germany, Greece, Hungary, Iceland, Ireland, Israel, Italy, Japan, Korea, Latvia, Luxembourg, Mexico, the Netherlands, New Zealand, Norway, Poland, Portugal, the Slovak Republic, Slovenia, Spain, Sweden, Switzerland, Turkey, the United Kingdom and the United States. The European Union takes part in the work of the OECD.

OECD Publishing disseminates widely the results of the Organisation's statistics gathering and research on economic, social and environmental issues, as well as the conventions, guidelines and standards agreed by its members.

OECD PUBLISHING, 2, rue André-Pascal, 75775 PARIS CEDEX 16
(81 2017 05 1 P) ISBN 978-92-64-27225-5 – 2017